STEPPING STONES

God's Covenant Plan through the Ages

HEATHER L. CLAUSSEN

WESTBOW®
PRESS
A DIVISION OF THOMAS NELSON
& ZONDERVAN

Cover photo from Shutterstock

All Scriptures in this book are taken from the New American Standard Bible (NASB), copyright 1960, 1962, 1963, 1968, 1971, 1972, 1973, 1975, 1977, 1995 by the Lockman Foundation unless otherwise indicated.

Scriptures marked NLT are from the Holy Bible, New Living Translation, 1996, 2004 by Tyndale Charitable Trust and from Life Application Study Bible, copyright 1988, 1989, 1990, 1991, 1993, 1996, 2004 by Tyndale House Publishers, Inc.

Scriptures marked AMP are from the Amplified Bible, Expanded Edition, copyright 1987 by the Zondervan Corporation and the Lockman Foundation.

WestBow Press books may be ordered through booksellers or by contacting:

WestBow Press
A Division of Thomas Nelson & Zondervan
1663 Liberty Drive
Bloomington, IN 47403
www.westbowpress.com
1 (866) 928-1240

Because of the dynamic nature of the Internet, any web addresses or links contained in this book may have changed since publication and may no longer be valid. The views expressed in this work are solely those of the author and do not necessarily reflect the views of the publisher, and the publisher hereby disclaims any responsibility for them.

ISBN: 978-1-4908-3002-5 (sc)
ISBN: 978-1-4908-3001-8 (hc)
ISBN: 978-1-4908-3003-2 (e)

Library of Congress Control Number: 2014904803

Printed in the United States of America.

WestBow Press rev. date: 03/17/2014

CONTENTS

To my husband, Don,

my covenant partner for fifty-four years,

and to

my four children and their spouses,

and to

my twenty-one grandchildren

With special gratitude to my husband, Don, who first received the revelation of the covenants in the Bible and then shared it with me. He has been my teacher, my mentor, my adviser, and my counsel of wisdom. We have walked the way of the covenants together for many years, and I can't imagine any other way.

PREFACE

At the outset I make the declaration that the foundation for the beliefs and principles in this book are based on the Holy Scriptures, made alive by the Holy Spirit. Many theories, theologies, and interpretations of life can be offered to explain our existence on this earth. Years ago I hopped down a few of these rabbit trails myself, which seemed to make some sense at first but led to godless dead ends. The dubious conclusions were confusing, futile, and sometimes dangerous because the devil can gain a foothold of falsehood in some seemingly harmless philosophies. I am now convinced that the Bible is the truth—the only true resource for the revelation of who God is, who we are, and His incredible plan to save us from our independence and rebellion. For those of you who won't capitulate to one faith, who cannot be convinced that only one pathway leads to the true God, who cling to your own tolerant view of "all religions have truth in them and lead to the same place," I am curious as to what you teach your children. The Scriptures teach this in 1 Corinthians 8:5ff:

> For even if there are so-called gods, whether in heaven or on earth, as indeed there are many gods and many lords, yet for us there is but one God, the Father, from whom are all things and we exist for Him; and one Lord Jesus Christ, by whom are all things, and we exist through Him.

Perhaps you teach your children that all faiths are acceptable and tolerance is the highest virtue over all belief systems. When they grow up, they can choose for themselves, if they so desire, which faith makes the most sense to them. It seems to me that leaving them a legacy of tolerance for all faiths without teaching them about the one true God, who is the anchor to their souls, is setting them adrift in this turbulent and storm-tossed world. Some acknowledge that there is a God, but that He has not made Himself known and is unknowable. I have heard the premise that God set this world into motion but has nothing further to do with it and that we do not have anything to do with Him. We are under no obligation to this God.

In Acts 17, Paul stood in the midst of the Aeropagus and said,

> Men of Athens, I observe that you are very religious in all respects. For while I was passing through and examining the objects of your worship, I also found an altar with this inscription, "TO AN UNKNOWN GOD." Therefore what you worship in ignorance, this I proclaim to you. The God who made the world and all things in it, since He is the Lord of heaven and earth … He Himself gives to all people life and breath and all things; and He made from one man every nation of mankind to live on all the face of the earth, having determined their appointed times and the boundaries of their habitation, that they would seek God, if perhaps they might grope for Him and find Him, though He is not far from each one of us; for in Him we live and move and exist.

I refuse to erect an altar in my home with the inscription, "To an unknown god," and bequeath it to my children.

Some of you may declare that there simply is no god. Your philosophy of life regards religion and faith with disdain or condescension. Possibly you believe that you are here by happenstance and gladly take the reins of godship in your life to pursue ambition, education, achievement, pleasure, and entertainment. You run after whatever is attainable and appealing, according to your innate gifts and skills.

Or not. You need only answer to your own godhood and not to any higher power. Yet the apostle Paul presents a marked contrast to your view of life. He says that God has made Himself evident to you and made it plain in your inner consciousness. In Romans 1:20, he says, "For since the creation of the world His invisible attributes, His eternal power and divine nature, have been clearly seen, being understood through what has been made, so that you are without excuse." He also makes the statement in Romans 3:3 that "if some did not believe, their unbelief will not nullify the faithfulness of God, will it? May it never be!" When the end of life comes, according to your earthly view, that's it! The curtain falls on your godhood.

Will self-rule and godhood be your children's inheritance?

I have met many young people in recent years who seemingly are empty inside. They aren't rebellious, show no bitterness or unrest, and have no particular goals in life. I soon realized that conversations with them ran dry very quickly. After initial small talk about sports or their jobs, they have nothing from their souls, nothing of substance to offer. Occasionally I have asked them what they believe about God. Their usual answer is, "I don't know. I have never really thought about it." Then they shrug their shoulders and say, "I'm happy with my life the way it is."

However, our Good Shepherd is not happy when any of His sheep and lambs are lost. He is always calling for them, stirring a sense of yearning and lostness within them. Jesus said, "My sheep hear My voice, and I know them, and they follow Me; and I give eternal life to them, and they will never perish; and no one will snatch them out of My hand" (John 10:27). In the meantime, the god of this world is all too eager to offer them alcohol, drugs, sex, pornography, and any other addictions and distractions that prevent them from the possibility of yearning for their Shepherd and the terror of realizing they are lost. If we attempt to peek into the heart of the Father to understand how He feels when His sheep are oblivious to Him, these words give us a fairly good idea: "What injustice did your fathers find in Me, that they went far from Me and walked after emptiness and became empty?"(Jeremiah 2:5).

Is emptiness your legacy to your children?

For those of you who are devoted to another god other than the Lord Jesus Christ or to tenets and doctrines other than the Bible, these questions come to my mind: How does your god communicate his personal love to you, and how do you reciprocate your love? If you live by rules and dogmas set up by men (or one man or one woman) and strive to obey them every day by your own strength, effort, and determination, it seems that a perpetual burden has been placed upon you. If you do fall short, what happens to you? Who determines your right standing in your religion? Is your god alive?

Is a man-made religion your legacy to your children?

I would like to introduce you to a wonderful God who loves each of you so much that He died for you. He rose from the dead and is alive forevermore! By the shedding of His blood on a cross, He completed a covenant with His Father, and made a way for us to live on this earth in righteousness, peace, and joy. He has sent His Holy Spirit to help us, and He has set us free from the bondage of the law.

As far as I know, the Christian faith is the only faith that reveals the unfailing love of the Triune God—the Father, Son, and Holy Spirit. It is the only faith that offers forgiveness and a relationship of unconditional love with a God who is alive. When we enter into a relationship with Him, He converses with us through His revealed Word, through His Holy Spirit, through prophetic words, and through natural and supernatural circumstances. He wants us to talk to Him, cry out to Him, and worship Him.

We never can earn His love, and He never abandons us. This God has actually made a covenant with us through His Son, Jesus, and because He knows that mankind will sin and slip along the way, He has promised to fulfill both sides of the covenant, sealing it with an oath!

Walking in this covenant is the legacy I give to my children, my grandchildren, and my great-grandchildren.

If you believe that all pathways lead to God and that He is an unknown and unknowable God, if you do not believe in God, if you have never really thought about God and have ignored the stirrings within you, if your religion was established by a man or men who have placed the conditional burdens of obedience and performance on you to carry, if you are a Christian but have allowed the distractions and demands of this world to cause you to skim over the surface of your faith, I ask you to pause on the busy treadmill of life and contemplate the truths within this book.

Your children's legacy is at stake.

INTRODUCTION

Several years ago the Lord revealed the truth of the blood covenant in the Bible to my husband and me. At the time we had no understanding of the significance of God's blood covenant with us. As we began to study the Scriptures and ask the Holy Spirit to teach us, what we learned was life-changing. We knew we would never be the same again. Up to that time our Christian walk had been sporadic and incongruous, but as we began to understand God's covenant with us, it seemed as if all the pieces fell into place and the Bible made sense. It was an ongoing story about how our Creator made Himself known to humanity and then actually entered into an everlasting covenant with us!

It is probably safe to say that many people still do not know what a covenant is, let alone a blood covenant with God! The purpose of this book is to illuminate God's covenants to you and to give you clarity and insight into the way they are linked together to form an onward movement toward the ultimate miracle of mankind's salvation and reconciliation with the Father!

For starters, it is interesting that the Bible is divided into the Old Covenant (Testament) and the New Covenant (Testament). So many words could be used to define a covenant. Here is a simple definition: A covenant is the giving of my life and all that I possess to another while I receive the other person's life and possessions as my own. It is a mutual act, a formal act of committing ourselves to a binding, unbreakable relationship that is sealed in blood and ratified with an oath. This is the way that God expressed it: "And I will be their God and they shall be My people" (Hebrews 8:10). It is a relationship of loyalty and love. Our God's eternal desire is for all of us to become sons and daughters to Him by covenant. What a gracious and wonderful God we have! Our understanding of the Blood Covenant is crucial to our faith.

As you read this covenant history, I pray that the Holy Spirit will open your hearts and eyes to see the faithfulness and lovingkindness of our God even when His people were unfaithful and broke the covenant. Our faith has the benefit of hindsight now as we look back over the thousands and thousands of years of history. God's track record is flawless. As 1 Kings 8:56 says, "Not one word has failed of all His good promises." We can only conclude that what He promises, He will do. One of the challenges of this covenant story is whether we will trust Him, like Moses and David did, even when the answers to our prayers are not immediate.

Covenants in the Bible always included the shedding of blood. In these chapters, look for the trail of blood that winds its way from the Garden of Eden (when God sacrificed animals for skins to cover the sin of Adam and Eve) to the unimaginable blood covenant He cut with Abraham to the crucifixion of Christ to the book of Revelation, when John saw a Lamb standing, as if slain, in heaven. In the book of Leviticus we are told that "life is in the blood" and is therefore highly valuable to God. The blood from the sacrificial animals that atoned for the sins of the people finally led to the precious and powerful blood of Jesus Christ, which eradicated sin and put an end to sacrifices once and for all. When we realize that all of this, even the death of Jesus, was the master plan of God from before the world began, we should fall on our knees before Him!

Also keep in mind that this book contains the historical sequence of the covenants, almost like connecting the dots of God's eternal plan. He chose a man (Abraham), a people group (the Jews), and a nation (Israel) to be His very own. Tucked into this plan was God's desire all along for other nations to see the light of the chosen people, who were in covenant with the living God, and long for Him and the covenant. This desire of God's heart was finally realized when Simeon held the baby Jesus in His arms, prophetically blessed Him, and said, "A Light of revelation to the Gentiles, and the Glory of Your people Israel" (Luke 2:32). When Jesus came to earth, He declared, "I have other sheep that are not of this fold; I must bring them also" (John 10:16).

Finally it is my prayer that as God reveals Himself to you through the Scriptures, you will recognize Him as a family God as well as a covenant God. At the outset when He put into motion His divine plan of salvation through the covenants, He made a covenant with families. Whenever He bestowed His covenant promises to a man in the Bible, such as Noah or Abraham, He always included the man's children, his descendants, and generations yet to come. He does the same for you and me. He wants to save whole families. Because of the covenant, families are one in His sight. You will see that He also used families as instruments of grace in carrying out His plans and purposes. Today He asks each of us to teach and lead our children to walk in this covenant with Him. It is our highest calling, and as we respond to this call, let our resounding cry be, "A Lamb for a house!"

CHAPTER 1

FROM EVERLASTING TO EVERLASTING

When I became aware that the Lord was asking me to write a book about His covenants with humanity and the involvement of families in His covenant plan, I was overwhelmed. It is a daunting challenge to grasp the heart of the infinite, omnipotent God, moving through the vast and immeasurable history of creation with a plan and a purpose. I wondered where I should begin. Then one day I heard Him say to me, "Begin at the beginning."

It is one thing to begin at the beginning, and quite another to begin "before the beginning!" Yet when I delved deeper into the Scriptures, I realized that the revelation of God *before* creation was more evident than I had remembered. In the past I must have glossed over a word like *everlasting* without dwelling on the profound meaning of the word. Passages in the Bible like Jeremiah 31:3 had seemed like beautiful, poetic language. "I have loved you with an everlasting love; therefore I have drawn you with lovingkindness."

Another example is Psalm 90:2. "Before the mountains were born or You gave birth to the earth and the world, even from everlasting to everlasting, You are God."

When I thought about eternity, my belief was based mostly on the biblical revelation of what happens when this life on earth comes to an end. I considered eternity to be a limitless future time in heaven in which we are living forever with the Lord. Then I came across this prophetic passage in Micah 5:2. "But as for you, Bethlehem Ephrathah, too little to be among the clans of Judah, from you One will go forth for Me to be ruler in Israel. His goings forth are from long ago, from the days of eternity."

Some of the language of the Bible is so deep and mysterious that we struggle to "get our minds around it," as they say. Yet once we accept the Scriptures as the Word of God, we have no choice but to read its lofty language and let its meaning seep into our spirits. I am referring to such verses as Isaiah 43:13, when the Lord declares, "And I am God even from eternity I am He."

At some point I realized that a *before* eternity is as evident in Scripture as an *after* eternity.

As we read these profound biblical revelations of a *before* eternity, we become aware of the truth that God existed in that everlasting eternity! Another way of saying this is to say that He *preexisted*. Colossians 1:17, in referring to Jesus, says, "All things have been created through Him and for Him. He is before all things, and in Him all things hold together."

When we contemplate the age-old question, "*Who* made all this?," we must come to the conclusion that the mystery of creation calls for a more complex response than simply replying, "God did it!" We will soon discover that the subsequent question is as laden with meaning as the first, "*Why* did God create the world?" When we delve into these fabulous and fathomless mysteries, we can only shake our heads and cry out, "God is awesome!"

One priceless strand of revelation reaching back to the *before* eternity is the Holy Covenant, which was intrinsic in the Trinity way back then. The Covenant of Oneness shared by the Father, Son, and Holy

Spirit even before creation is the ultimate model and expression of His everlasting love. It is a love that is indissoluble, indescribable, and eternal. God *is* love (1 John 4:8), and that love was pulsating and hovering as the Triune Deity in timelessness and space, even before the foundations of the world were laid.

Remember the verse in Genesis 1:2, "The earth was formless and void, and darkness was over the surface of the deep, and the Spirit of God was moving over the surface of the waters."

Even though the word *covenant* is no longer a common word or concept, we usually have a vague idea of what it is. In our modern age we think of it as a contract or agreement with promises and penalties attached, which isn't even close to the true meaning of a biblical covenant. Some religions, cults, and people groups, especially in the Far East, understand the concept of a covenant well because everything they believe and do emanates from the central core of their covenant and their subsequent responsibilities under that covenant. Although the covenants that still exist on this earth today are often sustained by their particular laws and rules with fear and bondage as results, I believe that the covenant that originated in the heavens with the Father, Son, and Holy Spirit has always been a relationship of absolute delight and joy! The finite mind cannot possibly comprehend the passionate and powerful love enjoyed by the triumvirate of the Eternal One, existing before time and before creation in unity and completeness. The Father, Son, and Holy Spirit exist in an unending covenant of love!

How can we know that? The only source of truth and revelation is the Bible, illuminated by the Holy Spirit, and as God's Word speaks to us, He asks us to accept this glorious disclosure by faith. As we have already noted, the eternal, everlasting love of God existed before time began. This love is spoken to us again in Psalm 103:17. "But the lovingkindness of the Lord is from everlasting to everlasting." Again in Psalm 136, the psalmist begins by proclaiming, "Give thanks to the Lord, for He is good, for His lovingkindness is everlasting," and repeats this declaration—"His lovingkindness is everlasting"—in each of the psalm's twenty-six verses!

It is crucial that we understand that the essential nature of God is unconditional love. If we can climb the edifice of faith to accept this revelation, we shall stand on firm ground, accepting the truth that God loved us, loves us, and will love us forever. Then everything else in the Christian faith will flow from that truth. In the wisdom of God He knew that we would need a further act to help us rest in the security of His love forevermore, so incomprehensibly He invited us to share in the holy covenant of the Godhead!

Jesus also has given us some long glances into the love He shared with His Father in the *before* eternity. In John 17:24, He prays, "Father, I desire that they also, whom You have given Me, be with Me where I am, so that they may see My glory which You have given Me, for You loved Me before the foundation of the world."

In John 16:5, Jesus prays, "Now, Father, glorify Me together with Yourself, with the glory which I had with You before the world was." Jesus also promises the coming of the Holy Spirit in John 15:26, "When the Helper comes, whom I will send to you from the Father, that is the Spirit of Truth, who proceeds from the Father, He will testify about Me." In John 16:28, Jesus says to His disciples, "I came forth from the Father and have come into the world; I am leaving the world again and going to the Father."

Once I understood the *before love* of God, these verses made more sense than ever before. They testify to the Covenant of Three, which is eternal and ongoing, and in this age it has been offered to the world, if the world would receive it. What a thought! All we need to do is receive it!

4

Malcolm Smith has taught about God's covenant for years. He is an excellent teacher on the subject. In his book *The Lost Secret of the New Covenant,* he defines a covenant as the giving of one's whole person and life to another and the receiving of that other person's life as yours. A covenant is a binding, unbreakable obligation between the parties. It is a giving away of oneself. This is exactly what God did, Malcolm Smith says, asserting that He decided to include His future creation, including humankind, who was yet to come, into His Holy Covenant. His unconditional love and the strength of that love initiated this decision. Malcolm Smith points out that God was under no constraint to do this but desired and chose to give Himself away because the love and joy He had experienced in the Triunity in the heavenlies was just too good to keep to Himself![1]

This we know from Revelation 4:11: "Worthy are You, our Lord and our God, To receive glory and honor and power; for You created all things, and because of *Your will* they existed, and were created."

We need to keep in mind that God planned and intended that we would have a relationship with Him. He wanted us to be His sons and daughters. This is why God said, "Let Us make man in Our Image, according to Our likeness" (Genesis 1:26). God wanted a family to share in the love relationship of His Holy Trinity family. It reminds me of our marriages here on earth. When a man and woman love each other and marry, they usually begin to desire a family extending their love to offspring. It is a natural desire written into the spirits of men and women from the beginning.

I hope that as we follow the covenants of God in this book, I pray that our heavenly Father will reveal His heart for families. He loves us. Not only did He include humanity in His eternal family, but He also unveiled a wondrous plan for us to reproduce ourselves so that He could have many sons and daughters through the ages. He chose to accomplish this through earthly families and through generations.

He also desires in His heart to draw people into oneness with Himself and with one another, thus answering the prayer of Jesus "that they may be one even as we are" (John 17:11).

In order for God to bring earthly families into reality, He first needed to create an environment in which they could live and move and have their being, and the resulting world is all around us! He didn't need to make it so marvelous and beautiful, so varied in its terrain and detailed design, so spectacular in its scope, but there is no other conclusion we can come to than the fact that He did it for us, out of His heart of unconditional love. We certainly don't deserve the grandeur that we see every day and every night. As the psalmist says in Psalm 8:3, "When I consider Your heavens, the work of your fingers, the moon and the stars, which You have ordained; what is man that You take thought of him, and the son of man that You care for him?"

The answer to that question is that we are sons and daughters of the Most High God and He created the heavens and the earth and all that is in them for us because He loves us!

So God gave Himself away and said, "Let there be—"

Let There Be

When foundations of the earth were laid
and even before,
did You, the Eternal Three,
move through the amorphous mists
and dance upon the darkness of the deep
in ecstasy of being one?

When morning stars rejoiced and sang together,
was Your love complete in covenant,
and yet welled up within Yourself,
because You yearned to pour it out
on all creation yet to come
and families not yet born?

With love outflowing from Your oneness,
from Your Covenant of Three,
did You envision generations,
joined to Your Triunity—
In the mist and utter darkness
did You whisper, "Let there be"?

(HLC)

CHAPTER 2

FROM HEAVEN TO EARTH

Creation

Finally we have arrived at the beginning! The prelude to creation resounded with a preexistent love, and the strains of His eternal song will be heard until the end of time. God is always very intentional. This belief that God intentionally created mankind out of a heart of longing and love for us, choosing to include us in His preexisting Covenant of Oneness, negates all the other theories made by man about how this world came to be! If we meditate on His masterful plan and marvel at how perfectly all the principles and matter of the cosmos came together to sustain life, visible and invisible, we will find it difficult to acknowledge the theory that it was all due to a cosmic explosion called the "Big Bang" and that it ultimately just happened to fall into place. Put it this way: It would take more faith to believe that the elements of the universe were spinning and evolving through eons of time and that for uncalculated reasons and flukes at a certain point in time, they finally congealed and became our earth and everything in it than it does to believe that God spoke into existence the amazing statistics and magnificent wonders that make up our universe.

Some say that the number of stars in the heavenlies are equal to all the grains of all the sands on all the beaches of the world. Psalm 147:4 expands on that astronomical thought when it says, "He counts the number of the stars; He gives names to all of them!"

Since my family and I are residents of Minnesota, we should also mention the subject of snowflakes along with the stars and the sand! The Internet records the statistic that a single cubic meter of snow contains 360 million hexagonal, crystalline snowflakes and not one of them is identical! Each snowflake is unique, and each one is exquisite in its delicacy and loveliness. This is all the more amazing when we think of the deep blankets of snow that beautify our winter wonderland.

I take this opportunity to sound forth the Lord's declaration in Isaiah 45:18.

> For thus says the Lord, who created the heavens (He is the God who formed the earth and made it; He established it and did not create it a waste place, but formed it to be inhabited), "I am the Lord, and there is none else."

In these verses the Lord is emphatic that His act of creation is ample proof of who He is. He is asserting His identity through His creation and is making the further point that He did not create the earth as a waste place but formed it to be inhabited by us!

For those of us who are Christians and believe the words of Scripture about God creating the world because He loves us, I wonder how often we whisper, "Thank you," when we hear the gentle raindrops on our rooftop in the spring or speak out praises to the Lord when we gaze at a gorgeous sunset or give Him glory in our hearts when we watch a tiny ruby-throated hummingbird flit from blossom to blossom in the garden. All of creation is a gift to us from a God who loves us unconditionally. If we really believe this, we should be singing all the day long as in Psalm 95:2:

> Let us come before His presence with thanksgiving, let us shout joyfully to Him with psalms. For the Lord is a great

God and a great King above all gods, in whose hand are the depths of the earth, the peaks of the mountains are His also. The sea is His, for it was He who made it, and His hands formed the dry land. Come, let us worship and bow down, Let us kneel before the Lord our Maker.

Many of us are familiar with the first verse of the first chapter in the Bible, "In the beginning God created the heavens and the earth." Later in the chapter (Genesis 1:26) God says, "Let *Us* make man in *Our* image, according to *Our* likeness." This statement of Scripture points unmistakably to the fact that the Trinity, who was preexistent in eternity, was now involved in the creation. We know that the Father was a participant through the powerful words of His mouth. "Let there be—" He longed to have many sons and daughters to love, and He created the earth so that it would be a life-sustaining and beautiful habitation for us. Psalm 148 says, "For He commanded and they were created. He has also established them forever and ever." What about the other persons of the Godhead? Were they involved in creation at the beginning?

The answer to this question can be found in the first verses of the Gospel of John, referring to Jesus,

> In the beginning was the Word, and the Word was with God, and the Word was God. He was in the beginning with God. All things came into being through Him, and apart from Him nothing came into being that has come into being.

The Holy Spirit was already there. "The earth was formless and void, and darkness was over the surface of the deep, and the Spirit of God was moving over the surface of the waters" (Genesis 1:2).

Job 33:4 declares, "The Spirit of God has made me, and the breath of the Almighty gives me life."

The Father, Son, and Holy Spirit created this incredible habitation for us and then created humans, granting them a knowledge of what is known about God, for God made it evident to them.

> They know the truth about God because He has made it obvious to them. For ever since the world was created people have seen the earth and sky. Through everything God made, they can clearly see His invisible qualities—His eternal power and divine nature. So they have no excuse for not knowing God. (Romans 1:19–20 NLT)

As mankind has reveled in the grandeur of creation through the years, how many have been aware of the God who created it for them to enjoy? Across the globe in all manner of terrain and climate, people are partaking of the "earth and sky," as referred to in the Romans 1 passage. They are hikers, photographers, hunters, fishermen, travelers, pilots, joggers, rock collectors, bird-watchers, painters, scientists, doctors, sunbathers, mountain climbers, skiers, and campers. Do they see the artistry of God in each leaf and every feather of this beautiful world? When new parents gaze with wonder at their newborn, do they see the signature of the Creator written on their precious gift of life. Surely our Father in heaven is pleased when His people delight in what He has given them, even if they don't connect the dots from earth to heaven. Whether we acknowledge the Lord or not, the truth still stands that "every good thing given and every perfect gift is from above, coming down from the Father of lights" (James 1:17).

Marriage

Our Triune God formed man, the crown of His creation, of the dust of the ground and breathed into His nostrils the breath of life, and man became a living being. With each spectacular work of creation, God saw that it was good, and yet when He observed the man, His dearest achievement, He was not satisfied. He determined that it was not good for a man to be alone and proceeded to make a counterpart, a companion for him. God caused a deep sleep to fall upon the man, and while he slept, God took a rib out of his flesh and fashioned a woman. Remember that God is always intentional! What an ingenious idea to take the woman out of man, forever signifying their unity in marriage! Even though God chose to make each one in a different manner, each one was made in the image of God. These are the words of Genesis 1:27: "God created man in His own image, in the image of God He created him; male and female He created them." They would be *one*. Just as the covenant in heaven was three in one, this first marriage was three in one because the man and woman were united in covenant with each other and with their God. When Eve was presented to Adam, he said, "This is now bone of my bones, and flesh of my flesh; she shall be called Woman because she was taken out of man." The second chapter of Genesis ends with the statement that a man shall leave his father and mother and be joined to his wife and they shall become "one flesh." God blesses the unity of marriage.

To this day a bridegroom should receive his bride as from God's hand because she is chosen by God to perfectly complete him. The bride and bridegroom should be well aware that they are entering into a covenant created and established by God, with God as the third party. It is a covenant of oneness and cannot be separated. When we talk about covenants, we in America are not culturally familiar with what a covenant means. Yet most of us remember that in the past, traditional marriage was understood to be a solemn covenant sealed with vows in the presence of God. This understanding is taken from the account of the first marriage in Genesis but is fast fading away from our social and religious consciousness. As was stated earlier, God actually gave Himself away from His eternal entity in heaven to the sons and daughters He created on this earth. He expects us to do the same in a marriage covenant—to give our very lives and all

13

that we have to each other. I remember seeing a cartoon in which a pastor was speaking to the bride and groom as they stood before the altar in church. The pastor said, "You are supposed to say, 'I do,' not, 'I'll try!'" Our promises to one another have weakened almost to that level, as more than half of the marriages in the United States end in divorce. Few of us have been taught or can truly understand the depth of commitment involved in a covenant. We say, "Your life is my life," and, "My life is your life," but subconsciously we may think, *My life is my life.*

At the time of the creation of man, God had not yet taken on flesh, so the reference to being made in His image did not mean His physical image. Man and woman received the miraculous gift of life and reflected the glory of their Creator. Unlike all other created beings, the human race was endowed with spirit, reason, personality, intellect, emotions, character, morality, and the capability of loving and communicating with God and with one another. I believe that God, in His infinite wisdom and insight, perceived that in order for His nature and purpose to be revealed on this earth, it would take the combined expression of a male and female. God knew that Adam needed a helper to complete himself, one who was suitable to him for his daily work, for procreation, and for companionship. When a husband and wife functioned as a team, they accomplished God's purposes better than either one could alone. One of their prime purposes would be to model to their children the character and image of God. God knew it would take both of them to accomplish this.

Pause for a moment in your life and be filled with wonder at how God took a rib out of Adam's flesh and fashioned a woman in order to proclaim the message forevermore that a man and woman are to be *one* in marriage. Ponder with amazement how God originated and ordained the sexual and intimate act of marriage, which so graphically portrays that a husband and wife become "one flesh." The love of the spouses is sexually consummated, and the conception of children is accomplished through this act! Only God could have thought of that!

Procreation

If the unimaginable marital act of unity isn't enough to convince us of God's passion for a man and wife to participate in His covenant of oneness, what about the incredible event of conception, when the sperm of the father and the egg of the mother unite into one and a fetus begins to grow inside the mother's womb? The people of this earth seem to take this miracle in stride, and even little brothers and sisters do not seem unduly puzzled that a "baby is growing in Mommy's tummy!" God chose to reproduce mankind in this way, I believe, because it is an extraordinary and profound way to express His intentions for the oneness of the family covenant and, at the same time, His lovingkindness to each one of us! David sings out this sentiment in the poetic prose of Psalm 139:13:

> You made all the delicate, inner parts of my body and knit me together in my mother's womb. Thank you for making me so wonderfully complex! Your workmanship is marvelous—how well I know it. You watched me as I was being formed in utter seclusion, as I was woven together in the dark of the womb. You saw me before I was born. Every day of my life was recorded in your book.

Our nation debates the issue of when life begins, but it would be advisable for the debaters to read Psalm 139 and confront the truth that an embryo or fetus is being watched by God, as it is growing within the mother. These words are written in verse 16: "Your eyes have seen my unformed substance." Enough said.

A quote from King Solomon encapsulates this truth in Ecclesiastes 11:4. "Just as you do not know the path of the wind and how bones are formed in the womb of the pregnant woman, so you do not know the activity of God who makes all things."

How else could our Father in heaven reveal the astounding truth of *being one* than by implanting a child within the womb of a mother? The genes and DNA of the mother and father are interwoven into the unborn in secret, and at birth the physical characteristics of the parents are sometimes immediately identifiable. What a divine privilege it is to carry a child within the womb for nine months! It is sublime. It is an exalted state. A woman is filled up with the blessing of God and, in some way, experiences a pang of sadness when the baby is born and becomes a separate being outside her body. The Lord softens that *apartness* by the dependence of the newborn on the mother, nursing at her breast, preserving the oneness for as long as possible.

The family is God's masterpiece.

CHAPTER 3

FROM LIFE TO DEATH

Into the lovely, pristine paradise of Eden, where God walked in the cool of the day with Adam and Eve, conversing with them and loving them, two facts emerged that forever changed the course of God's perfect creation. A tree existed in the garden called the Tree of the Knowledge of Good and Evil. Because of this tree, we know that the potential for evil already existed in the Garden of Eden! We don't know when Satan was cast upon this earth, only that he was already there at the beginning. We have this reference to Satan's arrival in Isaiah 14:12, 13.

> How you have fallen from heaven,
> O star of the morning, son of the dawn!
> You have been cut down to the earth,
> You who have weakened the nations!
> But you said in your heart,
> "I will ascend to heaven;
> I will raise my throne above the stars of God,
> and I will sit on the mount of assembly
> in the recesses of the north.
> I will ascend above the heights of the clouds;
> I will make myself like the Most High."

In the New Testament, Jesus says, "I was watching Satan fall from heaven like lightning" (Luke 10:17). In the closing book of the Bible we again read this proclamation: "The great dragon was thrown down, the serpent of old who is called the devil and Satan, who deceives the whole world; he was thrown down to the earth, and his angels were thrown down with him" (Revelation 12:8–9).

This is another mystery in the annals of spiritual history, and since we are finite creatures, we have not yet mastered the incomprehensibility of the infinite realm. The only thing we know for sure is that Adam and Eve, who were created to be in covenant union with their Creator, to trust Him, and to have sweet fellowship with Him, were presented with a decision to make.

Another fact that became apparent right from the start is that God created man with a free will. Evidently automatons were not what God had in mind when He extended His covenant to His partners on earth! When we first pondered the longing in God's heart from eternity to share His love with sons and daughters, whom He would create in His image, we should have assumed that He desired to share His love with free beings. The interaction of love between them and their God would be a free choice. God chose choice!

Adam and Eve, our first parents, were presented with a colossal choice. Utilizing their free will, they affected the whole future of the human race! Adam's decision was not a solitary choice, but how could he have imagined the far-reaching effect of his choice? God had admonished the man to eat freely of any tree of the garden except for the Tree of the Knowledge of Good and Evil, for in the day that he would eat from it, he would surely die.

So the two things mentioned previously were put into action from the start—the introduction of evil and free will. Certainly one of the issues in the fall of man centered on the deception of Satan in the form of a serpent, who enticed Eve to eat of the fruit by suggesting to her that God could not be trusted. Satan lied to her and said, "You surely will not die. For God knows that in the day you eat from it your eyes will be opened, and you will be like God, knowing good and evil" (Genesis 3:4, 5). He was so crafty and sinister that he knew exactly where she was vulnerable, and his temptations were right on target. Isn't it amazing that he still does that today? The inherent irony is that they were tempted by the lie that they could be unfettered and set free to rule like God, and by succumbing to the lie, they became the slaves of sin.

It is a common understanding that what happened at the tree was a simple act of disobedience. God made man in His image, which did not include rebellion or envy. Yet when Adam and Eve had everything they could ever want, when they were chosen to be included in the covenant of love by God, why did they choose to disobey? Eve believed the lie of the serpent.

Eve saw that the tree was good for food, that it was a delight to the eyes, and that it was desirable to make one wise. So she took from its fruit and ate and gave it to her husband with her, and he ate.

As Adam and Eve stood before that tree, it was a "make it/break it" moment. What did they make by eating of the forbidden fruit? They had hoped to be like God and make their own way from that day forward. What did they break by this decision? They had broken the covenant of union with God, for which they had been created. They turned their backs on the covenant, declared their independence, and disconnected with the only true life-source there is—the life of God. And mankind has done just that in the thousands of years since. This condition is spelled out in Isaiah 53:6, "All of us like sheep have gone astray, each of us has turned to his own way." God's response to this decision was and is this:

> But my people have changed their glory for that which does not profit. Be appalled, O heavens, at this, and shudder,

be very desolate," declares the Lord. "For my people have committed two evils. They have forsaken Me, the fountain of living waters, to hew for themselves cisterns, broken cisterns, that can hold no water. (Jeremiah 2:11–13)

What happened here has happened in every generation through the centuries. This is a message that is applicable now in this present generation! We could argue that Adam and Eve didn't really die or suffer any dire consequences from their disobedience. They lived a great many more years! The underlying truth is that they did die … spiritually. They no longer radiated the image of God and could no longer reflect His glory. They had pulled the plug on their life source. It is still a great deception in our day. It is possible for us to feel alive and well in our bodies, emotions, and thoughts and be well-liked and sociable, but in reality, we are *dead* because we have connected to a counterfeit life source. If you approached a man on the street and asked him, "Are you alive?" he would think you were crazy. The natural man considers himself to be made up of body and mind, which are obviously alive! Yet, if he has ignored the covenant of God and has refused or neglected to hear the truth of who he is and who God is, his spirit is dead!

Many people of this world dig into the wells of their physical existence for the meaning of life. Some merely exist, not digging or drinking from any well in particular. Mankind is either alive with the life of the only true God or dead spiritually. In John 10:10, these are the words of Jesus: "I came that they may have life, and have it abundantly." Even the church can be alive with the life of God or dead spiritually! In the final book of the Bible Jesus addresses the church in Sardis, "I know your record and what you are doing; you are supposed to be alive, but (in reality) you are dead. Rouse yourselves and keep awake, and strengthen and invigorate what remains and is on the point of dying" (Revelation 3:1–2) Paul used similar words when he wrote to the Ephesian church, "Awake, sleeper and arise from the dead, and Christ will shine on you" (Ephesians 5:14).

It may seem unjust that "through one man sin entered into the world, and death through sin, and so death spread to all men because all sinned" (Romans 5:12). Yet we guard our free choice at all cost and resist being dependent on God through the covenant just like Adam did. We are a "far cry" from the creatures God created us to be. Even though we may know the truth, we pursue many broken cisterns that can hold no water, and our lives can become pointless and empty. We may not think it is fair that we inherited Adam's old nature, which continually rears its ugly head, but it *is* fair that we are responsible for our own sins. God has free choice too, and He has chosen to allow Adam's DNA to remain in us and through us to the present day. Through Hosea, God says, "Like Adam they have transgressed the covenant; there they have dealt treacherously against Me" (Romans 6:7).

Have you ever wondered why God didn't make more Adams and Eves at the beginning? Maybe one of them would have said yes to the covenant and trusted in God and no to independence and self-rule! The answer probably lies in the fact that one God created one man and that we are all from that one God and one man, following the lineage of the human family from generation to generation. All of us have one Father, and it is quite evident that He has had oneness and unity in His plan from eternity. We are one blood and family members of the household of God!

Needless to say, Adam and Eve committed a monumental error. The sublime utopia of Eden was shattered, and nothing was ever the same again. Because the glory that had clothed them had disappeared, husband and wife sewed together some fig leaves to cover their nakedness. They were making an unsuccessful attempt to hide themselves and their sin. At this point God intervened and provided clothes for them from the skins of animals. Adam and Eve must have looked on in astonishment and horror at the spectacle of animals being put to death and the shedding of the first blood ever to cover their sin. Because of their disobedience, our first parents on this earth became aware of the concept of sacrifice and that the blood of an animal dying in their stead provided an atonement for sin.

This time marks the beginning of the concept of the Blood Covenant. In fact, from this time forward a trail of blood begins to form, winding its way through the generations. This scarlet cord extends from the sacrificed animals in the Garden of Eden to clothe Adam and Eve with skins to the blood of the innocent Lamb of God, which was shed to clothe all who come to Him with robes of righteousness. The lovingkindness and faithfulness of our God are the unfailing factors throughout the journey to fulfill His plan to bring salvation to all mankind.

God also pronounced some consequences and curses for what Adam and Eve had done, which have affected us and our world to this day. Yet in the midst of this scene of despair God declared a prophetic promise of hope to sinful man, disclosing His unchanging, unconditional love and His far-off plan of salvation. He said to the serpent, "And I will put enmity between you and the woman, and between your offspring and hers; he will bruise your head, and you will bruise his heel" (Genesis 3:15).

These words affirm that God's intent was to keep His covenant with Adam and Eve and with all their descendants. Though man had chosen to break the covenant, God was faithful, and in the framework of the covenant He would carry on because He could not deny His very nature. He would send One, the offspring of the woman, who would ultimately and eternally defeat the serpent.

Did God know that this disaster of disobedience in the Garden of Eden would happen? Did He have the foreknowledge in eternity that man would turn his back on His covenant and need a savior? When He gave the indescribable gift of creation to us, did He also predetermine in His heart to give us the unspeakable gift of His Son? Yes.

The Scriptures attest to the foreknowledge of God and His provision to cover the sin of man by the sacrifices of animals in the Old Covenant and finally in the ultimate sacrifice of His Son, Jesus, in the cutting of the New Covenant.

In Acts 2:23, Peter addresses the people of Jerusalem on the day of Pentecost, "This Man, delivered over by the predetermined plan and foreknowledge of God, you nailed to a cross by the hands of godless men and put Him to death."

In 1 Peter 1:18, he again states,

> You were not redeemed with perishable things like silver or gold from your futile way of life inherited from your forefathers, but with precious blood, as of a lamb unblemished and spotless, the blood of Christ. For He was foreknown before the foundation of the world, but has appeared in these last times for the sake of you.

Jesus knew He was destined for the cross before He created us, and yet He created us! His love for us caused Him to pay the highest price that heaven and earth had ever exacted. He was willing to pay the cost. That searing, swirling love that He had shared in the eternities as the Triune God was now poured out with passion on the cross for us.

This verse in Revelation 13:8 always amazes me:

> All the inhabitants of the earth will worship the beast—all whose names have not been written in the Book of Life belonging to the Lamb that was slain from the creation of the world.

God knew all along.

CHAPTER 4

FROM FREEDOM TO SLAVERY

Going It Alone

As the curtain fell on the fall of man, the scene looked dismal indeed. Adam and Eve were banished from the Tree of Life and expelled from the Garden of Eden. As the cherubim and flaming sword were stationed to guard the entrances to the Garden and the Tree of Life, they walked out into a world of thorns and thistles. They had discarded the covenant with God as a necessary life source and chosen instead to be independent, with the belief that they could dig up and derive their life source from many broken cisterns. They had chosen to do life on their own!

Whether they realized it or not, they had pioneered a counterfeit way of life and would pass that deception down to their descendants from generation to generation. They must have felt a sense of liberation in that they no longer needed to answer to God, and yet at the same time they must have discovered that life is hard when you go it alone. In striving to be free from the rule of God, they became enslaved to sin and Satan. They soon experienced sweat, toil, the pain of childbirth, and eventually … physical death. Since they were created to find their meaning in the God of the covenant and His unconditional love, they must have found their pursuit of false meaning frustrating and futile. The truth of the matter is that the condition of man has not improved as the years have gone by.

We have all inherited the sinful nature of Adam and Eve, and left to ourselves, we make the same sinful choices they did by saying no to God and yes to the lie of Satan. God laments this unchanged choice of mankind in Jeremiah. "My people have changed their glory for that which does not profit" (Jeremiah 2:11). "Why do My people say, 'We are free to roam, we will no longer come to You'?" (Jeremiah 2:31).

Another powerful proclamation from the mouth of God for the ages appears in Jeremiah 2:19. "Know therefore and see that it is evil and bitter for you to forsake the Lord your God."

As we contemplate this disappointing beginning of our history, we need to also remember the lovingkindness of our God. Despite His broken heart, He already had a master plan in motion.

The Family

One of God's brilliant ideas, which would involve His covenant and the salvation of man, was the extension of His human creation by means of the family and generations. The family became a means of grace. After He created Adam and Eve, God blessed them and said to them, "Be fruitful, multiply, and fill the earth" (Genesis 1:28). We saw how God created the covenant of marriage by taking the rib out of Adam and making a woman to depict the oneness of marriage. Adam said, "This is now bone of my bones and flesh of my flesh. She shall be called 'woman' because she was taken out of man" (Genesis 2:23). Just as Adam and Eve were one in the nuptial vows before God and in the consummation of the sexual act, becoming one flesh, so their progeny would be one, as the covenant was extended. Can a husband and wife who are in a spiritual covenant with themselves and their God stand on the truth that the children who issue forth from their union are also in the covenant of oneness? I realize that some who read this will say, "I thought God created us with free will, and when my children reach maturity, they can choose for themselves whether or not to enter the covenant."

I am basing my question on the divine plan and purposes of God. It is God's will that a man and woman become one flesh and *vow* to fulfill the terms of the covenant. It is also God's will that a man and woman *obey* the terms of the covenant and work out their oneness by day-to-day adherence to the Word of God and the revelation, direction, and help of the Holy Spirit. The bar has been set very high, according to Paul, when he says this about the marriage union:

> For this reason a man shall leave his father and mother and shall be joined to his wife, and the two shall become one flesh. This mystery is great; but I am speaking with reference to Christ and the church. (Ephesians 5:32)

This was God's intention: A husband and wife were to represent Christ and His church. A father and mother were to represent God to their children.

Because we have inherited our independence from Adam and Eve and because of the temptations from Satan and the world system, which entice us to partake of its pleasures and to search elsewhere for significance, it isn't easy! The same truths that apply to our marriages also apply to our families. God sees our families as one and longs for whole families to be saved and to come to the knowledge of the truth. This is His heart. This is His desire from before the foundations of the earth were laid! What a mandate this is for us to raise our children to choose life, which is truly *life!* In John 10:10, Jesus says, "I came that they may have life, and have it abundantly." How crucial it is to teach our children that any life source that seems to offer meaning and fulfillment apart from the life source of our Covenant God is a lie of Satan! How we need to represent our God to our children! God needed both male and female (made in the image of God) to complete a picture of Himself to them, combining the balance of nurturing love and discipline, of tenderness and strength of character.

Look at these words from Malachi 2:14–15 AMP.

> Yet you ask, Why does He reject it? (The offering) Because the Lord was witness (to the covenant made at your marriage) between you the wife of your youth, against whom you have dealt treacherously and to whom you were faithless. Yet she is your companion and the wife of your covenant (made by your marriage vows.) And did not God make you and your wife one flesh? Did not One make you and preserve your spirit alive? And why did God make you two one? Because He sought a godly offspring from your union. Therefore take heed to yourselves, and let no one deal treacherously and be faithless to the wife of his youth.

Though mankind broke the covenant with God, He did not break His covenant with them. As we saw before, He offered a prophetic promise in the presence of the serpent. "And I will put enmity between you and the woman, and between your offspring and her Offspring." From this time forward, creation could dare to hope that their God of wisdom and love had a plan of salvation that would eventually deliver such undeserving beings as themselves from everlasting destruction. I hope you can catch a glimpse of the stroke of genius that shone with brilliance on darkened and dismal humanity in the immediate and ongoing entity of the family, through which God would work until the end of time! It was a way and a means for Him to pour out His lovingkindness from generation to generation.

Have you noticed how the sinful nature of man only gets worse? I have often wondered how evolutionists can project their theories about mankind continually evolving into better, more knowledgeable, more capable, more sophisticated creatures. They must look at the moral depravity of our world and the striking resemblance to Sodom and Gomorrah, deleting it from their computer/brain cognizance!

After Adam and Eve were expelled from the garden, it is amazing how quickly their sinful DNA manifested itself through their children. Their first son, Cain, committed the first murder. In a jealous rage he shed the blood of his brother because God had accepted Abel's offering of a firstborn lamb from his flocks and had rejected Cain's offering of crops from his harvest. Since God created life (and Leviticus 17:10–14 states that "life is in the blood"), only God has the authority to take life away. It became apparent that man would continue to take things into his own hands and act independently of God. Yet, despite the headlong fall of mankind, one thing was still preserved—his free will. Throughout his existence on earth, men would battle sin from the inside and from the outside. Yet he could still choose to do right or wrong. God had spoken to Cain before he killed his brother and said,

> Why are you so angry? Why do you look so dejected? You will be accepted if you do what is right. But if you refuse to do what is right, then watch out! Sin is crouching at the door, eager to control you. But you must subdue it and be its master. (Genesis 4:6–7 NLT)

God gave Cain a chance to right his wrong. He still had the free will to choose to obey but chose to disobey. On the other hand, thousands of years later we read these amazing words in Hebrews 11:4: "Abel's offering gave evidence that he was a righteous man, and God showed His approval of his gifts. Although Abel is long dead, he still speaks to us by his example of faith." We learn that Eve had another son, whom she named Seth, because she said that God had granted her another son in place of Abel. "When Seth grew up, he had a son and named him Enosh. At that time people first began to worship the Lord by name" (Genesis 4:26).

Although fellowship with God was broken along with God's heart, the clear choice of obeying or disobeying Him remained. Good and evil continued to coexist. As time went on, however, it became apparent that the people of the earth, who were created in the image of God and were included in the covenant of heaven, continued to choose their own way rather than God's way. A web of evil seemed to be cast over the earth, and it permeated the hearts of men. As we follow the narrative of the Bible in Genesis, we can't help but observe that "evil breeds evil." In Genesis 5:6, these sad words are recorded:

> Then the Lord saw that the wickedness of man was great on the earth, and that every intent of the thoughts of his heart was only evil continually. The Lord was sorry that He had made man on the earth and He was grieved in His heart.

The curtain falls on the corruption and violence of all flesh!

CHAPTER 5

FROM GENERATION TO GENERATION

The next chapter of Genesis opens by giving us the written record of Adam's descendants generation by generation and closes by informing us that a son named Noah was born to Lamech in the lineage of Adam.

About twenty-six genealogical lists exist in the Old Testament, with two generational lists appearing in the New Testament. Why did our God devote so much space and time in His Holy Word to these records of people who lived thousands of years ago? One reason is that the written record of genealogies was an important Jewish custom. The ancestry and bloodlines of the people were crucial for such matters as inheritance rights, the apportioning of land, the heirs to the throne, and the lineage of the priesthood. Some of the accounts include names, births, life spans, and descendants as far back as seven generations. The annals of the genealogies established Jewish history and an accurate chronology of events.

> Know therefore that the Lord your God, He is God, the faithful God, who keeps covenant and His lovingkindness to a thousand generations with those who love Him and keep His commandments. (Deuteronomy 7:9)

Above and beyond the importance of generational chronologies for the Jewish people (and for all people) was that the promised Messiah would prove His validity through His lineage. In God's wisdom and knowledge He revealed and preserved an account of the generations to verify that Jesus descended from Abraham and David (the two men to whom the promise was made by God). Matthew makes this declaration in the first verse of the New Testament. "The record of the genealogy of Jesus the Messiah, the son of David, the son of Abraham," and he then proceeds to give the genealogy of Jesus. Scripture testifies to itself when it says that "all Scripture is inspired by God and is profitable for teaching, for reproof, for correction, and for training in righteousness"(2 Timothy 3:16) The generational lists are the Word of God! God has given us what we need from His depositories of knowledge to carry on His plan of the Holy Covenant by faith.

I believe that the genealogies in the Bible are essential, filled with truth, and laden with hidden treasures. Surely one of the intrinsic purposes of genealogies is to provide a covenant thread that extends from Adam to Jesus Christ to the end of the age. God chose the families and generations of the earth as a means of grace to lead us to the Savior promised in Genesis 3:15. "He is mindful of His covenant and forever it is imprinted on His heart, the word which He commanded and established to a thousand generations" (Psalm 105:8 AMP). "This will be written for the generation to come, that a people yet to be created may praise the Lord" (Psalm 102:18)

Wouldn't it have been far simpler for the Bible to contain statements like those in Matthew 1:17, "From Abraham to David were fourteen generations; from David to Israel's deportation to Babylon were fourteen generations; and from the deportation to the Messiah were fourteen generations," and leave it at that? He could have declared that twenty-six genealogies exist in the Old Testament (Covenant) and ended with "Amen." Again and again we are conscious of the truth that our Lord is intentional. He is relational and personal. He wanted to reveal to us that the names in the genealogies were real individuals who lived real lives and fathered sons and daughters who raised real families of their own.

As we read these numerous lists of generations that lived so long ago, we need to remember that God named the individuals then as He does now because He made each of us in His image. This is the hidden treasure of these enumerated names—that we are chosen, handpicked by Him to be His sons and daughters. This truth should give us immeasurable worth and dignity. In Ephesians 1:4, Paul writes, "He chose us in Him before the foundation of the world." From the eternities of eternities to the threshold of creation to the chronologies of the generations through all the centuries, He has called each of us by name. What an awesome revelation of truth! Isn't it amazing? Paul says in Ephesians 3:14, "For this reason I bow my knees before the Father, from whom every family in heaven and on earth derives its name."

The personal genealogies of our families here on earth are also important, if it is possible to research our generational histories. A relative of mine took it upon himself to compile a history and genealogy of my father's side of the family. In a large volume, which took him twenty years to complete, he published the story of the immigration of my great-great-grandfather, Johann, and my great-great-grandmother, Henrietta, from Prussia and their arrival in America in 1854. His book contains maps, pictures of their first farmhouse in Wisconsin, and their offspring. He follows the descendants with birth dates, marriages, children's names, and deaths to the sixth generation. God's plan for the perpetuation of the human race is the family and the covenant He has made with families. It gives us a sense of history, identity, and destiny. When I was asked about my heritage in the past, I would reply that my ancestors came from Germany (as Prussia was part of Germany), but as I pored through this book of my roots, I began to develop a profound respect and gratefulness for my forefathers and my foremothers! I have tried to put myself in the place of Henrietta, who, at thirty-four years of age, left her family and friends behind, never to see them again, and boarded a ship with Johann along with 647 other passengers, headed to a new country she did not know. She could not read or write and could speak no English. Yet they had faith in God, labored hard on their small farm in Wisconsin, and, years later, were able to give a farm to each one of their four sons as a wedding present! Because of the courage of my ancestors, I have enjoyed the innumerable blessings of growing up and living in this great country of America—the prosperity, the education, the religious freedom, and the privilege of sitting at my computer to write this book. As I followed my lineage through the generations, the realization came to me that nothing that happened in prior generations was by chance or inconsequential. I saw a picture of God's open hand extending over the epochs of time until it reached me and deposited into my life His gift of my heritage.

We live one generation at a time, but God oversees the vast span of generations. This is why it is important to study the genealogies of the Bible and our own personal genealogies so that we can perceive God's hand carrying out His plans among men. He is a generational God and often refers to Himself as the "God of Abraham, Isaac, and Jacob." He sees the big picture, and we are invited to take a look at it with Him. As we have seen, the worldview is this: "It's my life, and I am my own person. I am independent, and free to do as I wish." God's view is that we are in a covenant with Him and with our families, if we choose to accept His incredible offer. Even though He calls each of us by name and loves us individually, He considers us to be members of families that have existed over generations. "The counsel of the Lord stands forever, the plans of his heart to all generations" (Psalm 33:11).

Many blessings are passed on to us from our God and from our ancestors. If our ancestors lived in covenant with the true God, depended on Him, and derived their life source from Him, we will be drawn to His favor and lovingkindness. It is also possible for the iniquities of our fathers to be visited on the children and on the grandchildren to the third and fourth generations! This is best described in this verse from Exodus 34:6:

> The Lord, the Lord God, compassionate and gracious, slow to anger; and abounding in lovingkindness and truth; who keeps lovingkindness for thousands, who forgives iniquity, transgression and sin; yet He will by no means leave the guilty unpunished, visiting the iniquity of fathers on the children and on the grandchildren to the third and fourth generations.

In His great mercy God has revealed that we may have a disposition for or are susceptible to taking on the sins of our fathers and mothers and the sins of our grandfathers and grandmothers and even ancestors before that! Because of His lovingkindness, He warns us to identify the sinful propensities and traits that are handed down the family line. Just as we might have cried out, "It's not fair!" when we realized that we inherited Adam and Eve's sins of disobedience and independence, so we could cry out with the same cry when we learn that generational sins have been handed down and landed on us, making us prone to partake of the same sins. How can we be affected by the sins of our forefathers when we didn't even know them or much about them and didn't commit their personal sins? Our first impulse from a worldly view is probably to cast a glance at our preceding generations from afar and to regard them as having very little to do with us and our everyday existence.

We need to look at this revelation once again from God's viewpoint and be reminded of His perspective on the family. He created us and considers each of our families and generations on the earth to be one, to be in covenant with Him and with one another. This means we are recipients of both the blessings and the iniquities. Although the "passing down of iniquity" attracts us to a certain area of sin, it does not force us to sin. We still have free will!

I am fascinated by the unique abilities people have been given, such as the musical talent of a concert pianist, the genius of a scientist or engineer, the natural skills of an accomplished athlete, the intellect of a mathematician, or an artist's awe-inspiring painting. All of these gifts and thousands more have been inherited from our ancestors. When God has placed us in a family line to receive a particular gift, we are happy to receive it and usually work diligently to perfect it. Yet we often ignore or deny the iniquities that also come down through the family line.

When a revelation such as this comes from God, He always provides a way and means to help us. His motive is never to condemn us or to weigh us down with hopelessness and guilt. He desires to cleanse us and bless us.

> Behold, the Lord's hand is not so short that it cannot save; nor is His ear so dull that it cannot hear. But your iniquities have made a separation between you and your God, and your sins have hidden His face from you so that He does not hear. (Isaiah 59:1–2)

This verse from Isaiah could be indicative of why some of our prayers are not answered! What mercy and grace God is offering us by showing us the way to cleanse our family lines from the sins of our ancestors as well as our own sins! The first step we need to take is to agree with God's viewpoint on the "sins of the fathers." Looking at our generations through His eyes, we will see that we are one because of the family covenant. We can no longer look back on our heritage with indifference and aloof independence. Our attitude should be one of gratefulness for the good gifts we have inherited and a resolve to cooperate with God in cleansing our family line from all iniquity. We know we are recipients of God's lovingkindness, but we also know that God is just. In Leviticus 26:40–42, we are told what to do next.

> If they confess their iniquity and the iniquity of their forefathers, in their unfaithfulness which they committed against Me, and also in their acting with hostility against Me ... or if their uncircumcised heart becomes humbled so that they then make amends for their iniquity, then I will remember My covenant with Jacob, and I will remember also My covenant with Isaac, and My covenant with Abraham as well, and I will remember the land ... When they are in the land of their enemies, I will not reject them, nor will I so abhor them as to destroy them, breaking My covenant with them; for I am the Lord their God. But I will remember for them the covenant with their ancestors, whom I brought out of the land of Egypt in the sight of the nations, that I might be their God. I am the Lord.

This promise from Leviticus is a helpful model for us to use when we confess the sins of our ancestors and confess and repent of our own sins. It gives us an inside view into God's heart and holiness. We know He is faithful to forgive and to cleanse us from all unrighteousness. When He sees a humble heart, He remembers His covenant to all generations! As the Holy Spirit helps us, our family line can be purged of all iniquity from the past and on into the future! What a powerful weapon to defeat the devil and set our families free!

The good news of the gospel is that although we, "like sheep, have gone astray, the Lord has laid on Him (Jesus) the iniquity us all" (Isaiah 53:5–6). In the New Testament (Covenant) Peter reminds us that we were "not redeemed with perishable things like silver or gold from your futile way of life, inherited from your forefathers, but with precious blood" (1 Peter 1:18–19). The blood of Christ saves us from the independent and empty pattern of ancestral sin, and all we need to do is confess the sins of our generations, repent of our own sins, and receive His forgiveness. We should boldly renounce the temptations that challenge us, the bondages that have entrapped us, and the weaknesses that make us vulnerable to the devil's attacks. It is of paramount importance to appropriate the finished work of the cross by faith, which is far more powerful than the intimidating power of the iniquities stalking us from our ancestral lineage.

In covenant oneness with the Triune God, in covenant oneness with our marriage partners, in pleading the covenant of oneness for our generations and our families, let's confess our sins, appropriate the blood of Jesus for our households, and close the door to the devil and his pattern of destruction through the years. The happiness and health of our children, our grandchildren, and our great-grandchildren depend on it! "Who has done this and carried it through, calling forth the generations from the beginning? I, the LORD … with the first of them and with the last … I am He" (Isaiah 41:4).

CHAPTER 6

FROM THE ARK TO THE ALTAR

When God first drew my thoughts into His thoughts regarding the human family and impressed on me that a deeper, more extensive, divine plan existed and wove its way throughout the course of the Bible, it was Noah and his ark that first attracted my attention. On the one hand, I was sorry that the Lord was sorry that He had made man (in Genesis 6) because He saw that the wickedness of man was great on the earth and every intent of the thoughts of his heart were only evil continually. On the other hand, I was hopeful because in this culture of corrupt unbelievers, Noah was a righteous man, blameless in his time, who walked with God. The issue that intrigued me was that when God told Noah that He intended to blot out man, whom He had created, from the face of the earth, He also promised to establish a covenant with him by saving him and his family in an ark that Noah would build according to God's instructions. Only Noah was set apart as a righteous man who obeyed God, and yet his family was included in this covenant. Did that mean that a family of that day followed the head of the family and, in the case of Noah, followed him into the ark? During the 120 years it took to build the ark, the New Testament records in 2 Peter 2:5 that Noah was a preacher of righteousness, warning the wicked of the coming doom, and yet it appears that he had no converts. The people of that day were unmoved and ignored his pleadings. Only he, his wife, his three sons, and their wives were spared (along with a menagerie of animals, of course). What about his wife, and what about his sons and their wives? Did they believe God? Were they converts? We will return to these questions later.

So the curtain rises again on God's creation after the fall, with the sights and sounds of violence and sinful pleasure permeating the atmosphere. Another sound, the sound of steady pounding can also be heard. It is the sound of Noah's hammer pounding wooden pegs into a mammoth ark.

Adam had alienated his relationship with God by disobeying His command and declaring independence from Him. He had also bequeathed his sinful nature to his descendants, and the people of Noah's day seemed to have reached a climax and culmination of this sad state. God was grieved in His heart over what people had done to themselves. He was sorry that the free will, which He had given so graciously to His creatures, who were made in His image, had been used to choose sin and death rather than life in a covenant relationship with Him. The difference between Noah and those who perished in the flood was their response to God's grace. God continued to show favor to those who had faith in Him, and obeyed Him. Noah pleased God and was a recipient of that favor. The Bible says that he walked with God. In fact, Noah was chosen by God to do a great work because he had faith that God would do what He said He would do in sending a flood to wipe out all flesh. As Noah subsequently obeyed God's detailed instructions in building the ark and filling it with animals and food, it was counted unto him as righteousness. This is how Genesis 6:22 ends: "Noah believed God and according to all that God commanded him, so he did."

God had already offered a covenant promise to Adam and Eve when He prophesied that the seed of the serpent would be crushed by the seed of the woman (Genesis 3:15). Now in the face of the terrible apostasy of man, the Creator of our souls purposed to rescue and preserve a remnant of His people from the defilement and corruption

40

all around. God's purpose in the flood was to destroy the wickedness and sin that permeated the earth.

Noah is sometimes called the "new Adam" or the second father of the human race. The contrast between Adam and Noah is that Noah and his family were sinful from the start. The inheritance of the fallen nature from Adam was inescapable and remains so today. Yet the covenant that God offered to Noah and his family was a new beginning. It was like starting over. In this new world, however, Noah and his wife were not alone. Their three sons, Japheth, Shem, and Ham, and their sons' wives were also with them.

The Ark

As in all covenants in the Bible, God Himself took the initiative from beginning to end. This divine judgment of the evil world was a portion of God's plan from the eternities, and His divine goal was to guide history toward the kingdom of God and His Christ. His idea of the ark was another one of His supremely remarkable ideas that has floated on the waters of the centuries to our very time. It has intrigued many people, young and old, believers and unbelievers, and explorers who are still looking for its remains in the mountains of Turkey. Yet, as Francis Frangipane reminds us in his article, "The Covenant Keeping God," it was not the ark that preserved Noah and his family from the flood but the covenant of God.[2] Every aspect of this endeavor was begun and finished by God Himself. He chose Noah to do this work on earth, gave him the specific instructions on how to build the ark, brought the animals to him, and closed the door of the ark.

The Rainbow

When the waters finally subsided and the ark came to rest on earth, God told Noah and his family to leave the ark and bring

41

all the animals out with them. Then God spoke to Noah and his sons and said,

> I establish My covenant with you; and all flesh shall never again be cut off by the water of the flood, neither shall there again be a flood to destroy the earth. God said, This is the sign of the covenant which I am making between Me and you, and every living creature that is with you, for all successive generations; I set My bow in the cloud, and it shall be for a sign of a covenant between Me and the earth. (Genesis 9:8)

When we carefully read these words in Genesis, we can ascertain that the rainbow in the sky would be a reminder to God as well as to all of us. God has revealed His Father's heart to us from eternity. Flowing out from the unchanging Covenant of Three in heaven was the longing to have many sons and daughters who were made in His image, included in this everlasting love! His passion and desire caused Him to first create a habitation for His people yet to come. Now as He regarded His world after the flood, He promised to never again cut off all flesh by the waters of a flood. In fact, it appears that this rainbow is primarily as a reminder for Him because He says in Genesis 9:14,

> It shall come about, when I bring a cloud over the earth, that the bow will be seen in the cloud, and *I will remember My covenant*, which is between Me and you and every living creature of all flesh; and never again shall the water become a flood to destroy all flesh. When the bow is in the cloud, then *I will look upon it*, to remember the everlasting covenant between God and every living creature of all flesh that is on the earth.

What should we be reminded of when we see a rainbow in the sky? Of course, we have the assurance that God will not cause a worldwide flood again on the earth or that "seedtime and harvest, cold and heat, summer and winter, and day and night will not cease, while the earth remains." When we see a rainbow in the sky, we should be reminded that God keeps His promises through all the thousands of years. Yet we should also be reminded that the flood at Noah's time was due to the horrible wickedness and violence of man and that God, who is holy and righteous, grieves over this sin-drenched earth now as much as He did in Noah's time. When I was accessing the Internet recently, searching for articles that might contain spiritual insight into the life of Noah, I was struck by the blogs that mocked the reality of Noah and his ark. The words were a vendetta not only against the reality of Noah but against the reality of God Himself! Nothing has changed since the time of Noah! Noah had 120 years to preach righteousness to the people of his day. Now centuries have passed, and the truth about God is still foolishness to those who are perishing.

What else should we think of when we see a rainbow in the sky?

These are the words of Jesus:

> For the coming of the Son of Man will be just like the days of Noah. For as in those days before the flood they were eating and drinking, marrying and giving in marriage, until the day that Noah entered the ark, and they did not understand until the flood came and took them all away; so will the coming of the Son of Man be. Then there will be two men in the field; one will be taken and one will be left. Two women will be grinding at the mill, one will be taken and one will be left. Therefore be on the alert, for you do not know which day your Lord is coming. (Matthew 24:36–42)

Be on the Alert

Be on the alert. If we really believe the revelations given to us through Noah and if we really believe that the coming of the Son of

Man will be like unto the days of Noah, it is up to us to bring the reality and righteousness of Jesus to our families first and then to all others who are put before us. Do our lives consistently express the love of Jesus and the power of the Holy Spirit to our families? Do our families believe that we truly hear the voice of God and therefore are willing to follow in our footsteps like Noah's family did? If we lead hypocritical lives, the power of our testimony will drain right out of us into the floodwaters! May the beautiful rainbow be not only a sign of God's side of the covenant with us but also our wake-up call to shake off our lethargy, to remember that He is returning soon, and to reach out to our families with a sense of urgency and desire to rescue them from this evil age.

The ancient account of Noah and his family gives us a graphic and indelible picture of the family covenant. Since Noah found favor in the eyes of the Lord, since he was a righteous man who was blameless in his time, and since he walked with God, the manifest fruit of his life was that his family also had faith in God and chose to be in the covenant. In the midst of a rebellious and riotous culture, his wife, his sons, and their wives believed that Noah heard the voice of God, and despite the clamoring all around them, they submitted to the task of building the ark. God told Noah, "I will establish My covenant with you; and you shall enter the ark—you and your sons and your wife, and your sons' wives with you." God was initiating a plan to destroy the detestable and heartbreaking evil of mankind, and yet He enclosed the family of Noah in the ark. The biblical account goes on to tell us that later when the ark had landed, God spoke to Noah and to his sons with him, saying, "Now behold, I Myself do establish My covenant with you, and with your descendants after you" (Genesis 9:9). God spoke to Noah and to his sons with him. God Himself accepted and blessed Noah's family. Remember when we looked at the importance of genealogies and the importance of each individual to God? God gave the ultimate gift of free will, and each individual must choose to relate to the Lord and enter

44

into a covenant relationship with Him. Yet at the same time the husbands and wives, the fathers and mothers, the grandfathers and grandmothers who are in covenant with God can contend daily for their children and grandchildren before the throne of God. They can model for their progeny the exemplary life that is possible because they are created in the image of God. Sometimes our children don't even know that there is a choice to make. Have we offered them the clear choice to say yes or no to God and to live in dependence on Him or to say yes or no to Satan and his lie, which is to live life on our own?

The Bible doesn't record that Noah and his wife had any more children. God chose Noah's sons, Shem, Ham, and Japheth, to repopulate the earth. The list of the genealogies of Noah's sons is sometimes referred to as the "Table of Nations" because from it we can determine which nations came from each of Noah's sons (Genesis 10:1–32). As God had told Adam and Eve to be fruitful and multiply, so He told Noah's sons to be fruitful and multiply.

Shem's descendants are listed in Genesis 11:10–26. Here are a few of his descendants who are of special interest because they link together the generations from Shem to Abraham.

10—These are the descendants of Shem.

24—When Nahor had lived twenty-nine years, he became the father of Terah.

25—And Nahor lived after the birth of Terah one hundred and nineteen years, and had other sons and daughters.

26—When Terah had lived seventy years, he became the father of Abram, Nahor, and Haran.

Shem lived long enough to be alive when Abram was born! Shem is the patriarch of the Israelites, God's chosen people. When Noah blessed Shem, he prayed that God would dwell in the tents of Shem. Shem's descendants were called "Shemites," which we now refer to as "Semites."

These genealogies are crucial to our understanding of how God's plan and intention continued to be accomplished through families and generations. Though He could see that all men were inclined toward sin and self-reliance, He still had a plan to bring them into oneness with Himself as He had intended from the beginning.

The Altar

When Noah could see that the surface of the ground was dried up, he went out with his sons, his sons' wives, and his wife. Every beast, every creeping thing, and every bird, everything that moves on the earth went out by their families from the ark (Genesis 8:18–19). As Noah stepped out of the ark, he must have been overwhelmed by the emptiness of the world around him and the enormity of the task that lay before him. Yet the first thing Noah did was to build an altar to the Lord, and from every clean animal and clean bird, which the Lord had commanded him to bring along, he offered burnt offerings on the altar. This act of Noah's certainly was a gesture of gratitude and worship to God for saving him and his family from the waters of the flood. Yet in reading this age-old story of Noah again and again, a strong, intuitive sense appears that he was acknowledging something more, something deeply spiritual on that altar. As he built this altar and sacrificed animals on it, I believe that God had revealed to him that the shedding of sacrificial and substitutionary blood was an essential element of the covenant that He was making with him. God had said in Genesis 6:18, "But I will establish My covenant with you; and you shall enter the ark—you and your sons and your wife, and your sons' wives with you." In Genesis 7:2, God had said to Noah, "You shall take with you of every clean animal by sevens, a male and his female; and of the animals that are not clean two." Why would God instruct him to include clean animals in the ark? It is important to keep in mind that Noah had found favor with God and walked with God. God had promised that He would never again destroy the whole earth because of the wickedness of man, but at the same time He must have disclosed to Noah that a plan was already in place for atonement and salvation. Psalm 25:14 says, "The secret of the Lord is for those who fear Him, And He will make them know His covenant."

God had revealed to Noah that the shedding of innocent blood was necessary for the covering over of the sins of the people so that the Creator could continue to have a relationship with His creation. Noah's act at the altar was a foreshadowing of the Blood Covenant God would make with Abraham and the ultimate and final sacrifice of Jesus Christ, the spotless Lamb of God.

The curtain falls as Noah sees the scarlet cord, and picks it up.

CHAPTER 7

FROM FAITH TO FAITH

As the curtain rises again on the storyline unfolding before us, we see an old man who is about seventy-five years old, trudging along the well-trodden ancient roads with an entourage of his wife and family members, servants, and animals, step by step, mile after mile, on a long, long journey. Where is he going? He doesn't know.

Just as Abram and his wife, Sarai, were slowly making their way along the road to their destiny, so was the sovereign God making His way along the road of history for the salvation of His people and the preparation of His kingdom. God, however, knew where He was going.

Despite the defection and apostasy of man, God remained faithful to the covenant He had initiated. We contemplated the unforgettable preservation of Noah and his family from the worldwide flood. We will now see another instance of God keeping His side of the covenant and at the same time providing for and working with His human counterpart on earth. I am reminded again of the words of Psalm 33:13.

> The Lord looks from heaven;
> He sees all the sons of men;
> From His dwelling place He looks out
> On all the inhabitants of the earth,
> He who fashions the hearts of them all,
> He who understands all their works.

God sovereignly chooses a man, calls him, fulfills His divine purposes through him, and accomplishes the impossible! What did these men possess that caused God to choose them? Some of the answers could be that He fashioned their hearts and understood all their works. They believed Him. They obeyed Him.

We have already established that Noah was a righteous man who walked with God, but surprisingly Abraham was from Ur of the Chaldees, which was a city and culture of idol worshippers and wickedness. Yet Hebrews 11:8 says this: "By faith Abraham, when he was called, obeyed by going out to a place which he was to receive as an inheritance; and he went out, not knowing where he was going."

We also should keep in mind that lineages, descendants, and families are very important to God since He is the one who preordained and planned the outworking of His human creation in this manner. Do you remember that after Cain killed Abel, God gave Adam and Eve another son named Seth? It is recorded in Genesis 4:25 that Eve named him Seth because she said, "God has appointed me another offspring in place of Abel." Chapter 4 then concludes that "men began to call upon the name of the Lord." Noah was a descendant of Seth, and this was an important factor in choosing Noah to do this great work as well as the trait that he was a righteous man. Abram was a descendant of Shem, Noah's eldest son. God chose Abram and, through him, chose a people for Himself. These chosen people would become a main constituent in the vast and predetermined plan of the salvation of mankind.

The scarlet cord of the blood covenant had been strung along the line of families and generations from Adam to Abram, and it would continue to follow the course of divine connection until the Messiah was born! It was the divine will and eternal decision of God that from Abram would come the Seed of the woman, which was prophesied in Genesis 3:15 to crush the seed of the serpent! It is inconceivable but true. Our Heavenly Father placed His Son into the lineage of mankind on this earth!

An interesting passage in Scripture in which God speaks about His choice of Abraham to be "His man" is found in Genesis 18:17.

> Shall I hide from Abraham what I am about to do, since Abraham will surely become a great and mighty nation, and in him all the nations of the earth will be blessed? For I have chosen him, so that he will direct his children and his household after him to keep the way of the Lord by doing what is right and just, so that the Lord will bring about for Abraham what He has promised him.

This appears to be almost a sneak peek into the divine heart of God and His purposes. It unveils His searing love and eternal call not only for each one of us but for our families as well. We need to continually be mindful of the most important assignment we have from God … to pass on the knowledge, wisdom, and ways of the Lord to the next generation. It is possible to accomplish great things in the eyes of men and history, to live and die and not even realize (or perhaps ignore) that we were chosen as God's first choice within the holy covenant to impart our faith and teach our households.

Years later Moses, the mouthpiece of God, passes on these instructions in Deuteronomy 6:6 from God to the children of Israel:

> Hear, O Israel! The Lord is our God, the Lord is one! You shall love the Lord your God with all your heart, and with all your soul and with all your might. These words, which I am commanding you today, shall be on your heart. You shall teach them diligently to your sons and shall talk of them when you sit in your house and when you walk by the way and when you lie down and when you rise up. You shall bind

them as a sign on your hand and they shall be as frontals on your forehead. You shall write them on the doorposts of your house and on your gates.

Wouldn't it be wonderful to have this be the epitaph on our tombstones when our lives on earth are done? "For I chose him, so that he would direct his children and his household after him to keep the way of the Lord by doing what is right and just!" May it be our legacy!

It is fascinating when we realize that from the very region where men gathered to build the Tower of Babel, God called Abram from the line of Shem, son of Noah, whose family worshipped false gods, to leave everything he had ever known and to go to a land he had never seen. How ironic that God proceeds to promise to Abram the very things the builders at Babel were trying to achieve before they were scattered over the face of the earth! They wanted a name for themselves. They wanted to be a great nation. When God called Abram, He said in Genesis 12:1ff,

> Go forth from your country,
> And from your relatives
> And from your father's house,
> To the land which I will show you;
> And I will make you a
> great nation.
> And I will bless you,
> And make your name great.

God is again asserting His godhood. He is putting mankind in his place. God is graciously giving to Abraham and His descendants what man wanted to achieve on his own for his own glory without participation from Him. Thank you very much! Our preeminent God had a magnificent, far-reaching, and unimaginable plan to restore humanity to covenant oneness with its Creator. He looked down from heaven to select a point man here on earth who would believe Him, obey Him, and begin to set His plan in motion, even though the man might not get the big picture. Most of us probably don't get the big picture when God asks us to do something. All He requires of us is to hear His voice and obey.

It will forever remain a mystery as to how Abram first encountered God in an idolatrous land and learned to recognize His voice. All we know is that "Abram went forth as the Lord had spoken to him" (Genesis 12:4). As he stepped out from all that was familiar and secure onto the road that led to a land he did not know, he placed himself in a position of absolute dependence on God! This act of obedience was the exact opposite of the mind-set of men since the fall in the garden, when Adam and Eve chose to live their lives independently of God.

Abram had followed the voice of God and put behind him his former life in Ur to go forth to an unknown land even before God had actually enacted a covenant with him. Abram responded to God from the beginning with a yes to all His invitations, commands, and promises followed by a remarkable and immediate obedience. Abram was confused, however, when God's promises included his descendants after him. God Almighty even changed Abram's name to Abraham, meaning "father of a multitude." Looking back at this incipient time, this crucial moment of prophetic declaration, we now know that Abraham is indeed considered the father of the Jews, the Christians, and the Arabs! In Romans 4:16, Paul says that the promise is guaranteed to all the descendants, not only to those who are of the Law but also to those who are of the faith of Abraham, "who is the father of us all."

Yet Abram was confused. In Genesis 15:2, he asks, "O Lord God, what will You give me, since I am childless, and the heir of my house is Eliezer of Damascus?" And Abram said, "Since You have given no offspring to me, one born in my house is my heir." Then behold, the word of the Lord came to him saying, "This man will not be your heir; but one who will come forth from your own body, he shall be your heir" (Genesis 15:4).

> And He took him outside and said, "Now look toward the heavens, and count the stars, if you are able to count them." And He said to him, "So shall your descendants be." (Genesis 15:5)

Typical of Abram, it is recorded that he believed the Lord, even though this dramatic proclamation was as unique and impossible then as it is now. This was almost as unbelievable as a virgin conceiving and bearing a child! Abram's faith was commendable, and it was reckoned to him as righteousness.

The Lord continued to proclaim that He would give all the land of Canaan to Abram and to his descendants after him. Abram passed through the land as far as the site of Shechem to the oak of Moreh. He could see that the warlike Canaanites were occupying the land (and it would take many battles for Abram's descendants to finally take possession of the land). At this promise Abram finally asked the question that we would probably have asked much earlier along the way, "O Lord God, how may I know that I will possess it?"

God could have been offended at this question. After all, it was God Almighty who was making these promises, incredible as they seemed. These words are written in Hebrews 6:13–20:

> For when God made a promise to Abraham, since He had no one greater by whom to swear, He swore by Himself, saying, "Surely I will bless you and multiply you." And thus Abraham, having patiently waited, obtained the promise. For

people swear by something greater than themselves, and in all their disputes an oath is final for confirmation. So when God desired to show more convincingly to the heirs of the promise the unchangeable character of His purpose, He guaranteed it with an oath so that by two unchangeable things, in which it is impossible for God to lie, we who have fled for refuge might have strong encouragement to hold fast to the hope set before us.

An Unconditional Covenant

When Abraham asked the question, "O Lord God, how may I know that I will possess it?" God proceeded to cut an unconditional covenant with Abram. An unconditional covenant is an agreement between two parties with only one of them required to do anything. The first part of this covenant, which was initiated and carried out by God, deals with the land promised to Abram. This blood covenant ritual was common at that time but usually involved two or more individuals or representatives of nations who entered into a covenant with one another. It was a very solemn pact because it involved the shedding of blood and a sacred oath. We should be aware that the connecting trail of the blood of the covenant is now being carried on through Abraham. Just as Adam and Eve marked the beginning of the trail when God clothed them with animal skins to cover their sin, Noah sacrificed clean animals to God on an altar before he did anything else. This scarlet line, or scarlet cord of the covenant now extends along the path of Abraham's life. It had become an established fact that the shedding of innocent blood was necessary so that God could continue to interact with His creation. Since God is a spirit and not flesh and blood, a substitute with blood needed to provide the necessary blood for the Blood Covenant. God made this covenant with Abraham and no one else. Later others entered into the covenant between God and Abraham through the rite of circumcision.

In Genesis 15:9, God told Abraham that he should bring a three-year-old heifer, a three-year-old female goat, a three-year-old ram, a turtledove, and a young pigeon. When these were brought to Him, they were cut in two, and each half was laid opposite of the other; however, He did not cut the birds. When the birds of prey came down upon the carcasses, Abram drove them away. This was about all Abram did in regard to partaking of this colossal covenant, for when the sun was going down, a deep sleep fell upon Abram, and a dreadful and great darkness fell upon him. Customarily the covenant participants began this ceremony by standing back-to-back in the center of the divided animals and then walking through the blood in the form of a figure *8*, to depict the unending nature of the covenant, a figure of infinity. As they walked, they would recite the terms of the covenant. They ended up facing each other in the middle, standing in the blood. The vow of the ancient ritual was that this was a covenant to life, and if either party broke the covenant, they themselves would die, as these animals had died.

However, God was the only speaker in this covenant with Abraham. He prophesied about the future of the children of Abraham and about the four hundred years they would spend in Egypt under oppression and slavery. He promised that He would deliver them from their captivity and bring them back to this promised land of Canaan. He also promised Abraham that he would die in peace and be buried at a good old age (Genesis 15:15).

Rather than including Abram in the covenant ritual, God alone passed through the pieces of the dead animals as a "smoking oven" and a "flaming torch." God said that Abram's descendants would be strangers in a land that was not theirs and would be enslaved for four hundred years. He promised that He would judge the nation that they served and bring them back to this land in the fourth generation when the iniquity of the Amorite was complete. So God made a covenant with Abram, promising the land to his descendants.

All of this was done by God's own initiative just as the creation of the world, and the creation of sons and daughters made in His own image were done by His own initiative. As God walked through these animal carcasses, He covenanted with Abraham that if these promises were not kept, He Himself would have to die!

This is an inconceivable grace, an incomprehensible grace, an amazing grace! It would be good for us to pause in our lives more often and immerse ourselves in these profound truths in the hope that some of them would sink in! The God of all creation stooped to cut a covenant with man because He loved us and was setting into motion an immense plan to redeem and reconcile us to Himself.

God promised Abraham that in his seed all the families of the earth would be blessed. This is huge! It was almost like promising Abraham the world! Actually it was the coming of the Messiah that blessed the world, and the Messiah came through the lineage of Abraham! We are the blessed recipients of this promise today, and this promise will go on and on until Jesus returns to establish His kingdom. In Acts 3:24, we read these words: "It is you who are the sons of the prophets and of the covenant which God made with your fathers, saying to Abraham, 'and in your seed all the families of the earth shall be blessed.'"

Long ago God proclaimed the good news to Abraham that all nations would be blessed through him. The Scriptures say in Galatians 3:9 that all who put their faith in Christ share the same blessing Abraham received because of his faith. How awesome is the lovingkindness of our God!

A unilateral covenant between two people of that day had certain rituals they shared. The participants of old exchanged vows and several other things to symbolize that everything they possessed (including their children) were freely given to the other. What a marvelous revelation that the God of the universe would willingly enter into a covenant (on His own initiative) with man! They customarily exchanged their cloaks, which was their personhood, and their belts, which contained their weapons (their strength). God had already appeared to Abram in a vision and said, "Do not fear, Abram. I am a shield to you" (Genesis 15:1).

They also exchanged their names. As mentioned before, God changed Abram's name from Abram (exalted father) to Abraham (father of a multitude). So Abram's name was changed because of its meaning, but God also saw fit to infuse His name into Abram's! God was known as Jehovah or YAHWEH. He breathed the *HA* sound of His name into Abram so that from that time on Abram became Abra'ha'm, and all who knew this knew that Abraham was in covenant with the Most High! God also took upon Himself the name of Abraham, and later when He confirmed His covenant with Isaac and Jacob, He was thereafter known as the God of Abraham, Isaac, and Jacob.

Sarai's name was also changed to Sar'ah'. Sometimes the importance of Sarah is overlooked because of the major, larger-than-life role of Abraham in the historical account of their lives. Here is what God said to Abraham:

> As for Sarai, your wife, you shall not call her name Sarai, but Sarah shall be her name. I will bless her, and indeed I will give you a son by her. Then I will bless her, and she shall be a mother of nations; kings of peoples will come from her.

Sarah, too, is a heroine of faith. She is mentioned in the "Hebrews Hall of Fame" in Hebrews 11:11. "By faith even Sarah herself received power to conceive, even when she was past the age, since she considered Him faithful who had promised."

The conception of a child in the womb of Sarah when she was ninety years old was supernatural. It was a miracle that birthed into motion the beginning of God's plan of salvation for mankind, which would provide the way for man to be restored to a relationship with his Creator. It is like a nugget of gold discovered in this incredible account that "by faith Sarah herself received power to conceive." How amazing it is to realize that God's whole future plan rested on Abraham, who believed Him, and Sarah, who "considered Him faithful who had promised!" This is the family covenant we are talking about. God is the one who chooses covenant partners and then equips them together to accomplish His purposes.

From the outset God had taken the initiative to enter into a covenant with Abraham. This is an unconditional covenant where nothing is expected of Abraham, and God fulfilled both sides of the covenant. God made this covenant not only with Abraham but also with his children and his descendants, even those who were yet unborn because they were in him.

Thirteen years later God appeared to Abraham again to reaffirm the covenant that He had made with him.

> As for Me ... I will establish My covenant between Me and you throughout their generations for an everlasting covenant to be God to you and to your descendants after you. I will give to you and to your descendants after you, the land of your sojournings, all the land of Canaan, for an everlasting possession; and I will be their God. (Genesis 17:7–8)

Circumcision

Up until now the covenant was unilateral, carried out by God without any requirements from Abraham. This time, however, when

God confirmed His covenant, He made a request on Abraham's part. He said to Abraham in Genesis 17:9–13,

> As for you, you shall keep My covenant, you and your descendants after you throughout their generations. This is My covenant, which you shall keep, between Me and you and your descendants after you: every male among you shall be circumcised. And you shall be circumcised in the flesh of your foreskin, and it shall be the sign of the covenant between Me and you. And every male among you who is eight days old shall be circumcised throughout your generations … thus shall My covenant be in your flesh for an everlasting covenant.

Every covenant had a witness or a reminder attached to it. This functioned as a perpetual reminder that the covenant had taken place. Sometimes it was commemorated by a stone marker or a heap of stones. The world remembers the covenant with Noah by the sign of the rainbow. In the case of Abraham, God asked that he and his descendants carry the reminder of the covenant in their own flesh. This particular reminder was unquestionably a seal of identity for God's chosen people. It was a token of their unique relationship with Him.

Yet the rite of circumcision seems like a bizarre request for God to make to Abraham. A sign of the covenant could have been affixed anywhere on the body like a piercing on the earlobe or lip or as a brand on the forehead. Could it be that God requested this particular reminder to be on the flesh of the foreskin of the male because that is where the seed is carried? One of God's great strokes of genius in creation is the progenitive aspect of a covenant marriage and the childbearing that comes forth from that relationship from generation to generation. I believe this request and reminder came right from His heart. Always and forever He is invested in His covenant with families.

It must have been quite a challenge for Abraham to gather all the males in his household and mandate them to submit to this very painful procedure. Yet the Scriptures are careful to record that on the very same day that God had spoken to him, Abraham was circumcised along with his thirteen-year-old son, Ishmael, and all the men of his household. Abraham was ninety-nine years old when he was circumcised. Now we can understand that one of the reasons God chose Abraham to become a great and mighty nation was that "he would command His children and his household after him to keep the way of the Lord (Genesis 18:19). Because Noah was a righteous man, his family trusted that he heard the voice of God when he built the ark. I believe that this was also true of Abraham. His household trusted that Abraham heard from the Lord. Do our households trust and respect that we hear from the Lord, especially if it requires a change in our lives and affects them?

Isaac

Perhaps the greatest test that Abraham faced was when God told him to sacrifice his son, Isaac. God said, "Take your only son, Isaac, whom you love, and go to the region of Moriah. Sacrifice him there as a burnt offering on one of the mountains I will tell you about." (Genesis 22:2). So Abraham rose early in the morning and set out on a three-day journey with Isaac and two of his servants.

When he and Isaac arrived at the place, Abraham built an altar and arranged wood on it. Then he bound his son, Isaac, and laid him on the altar on top of the wood. When he reached out his hand and took the knife to slay his son, the angel of the Lord called out to him from heaven and said, "Do not lay a hand on the boy, and do not do anything to him. Now I know that you fear God, because you have not withheld from me your son, your only son." Later Abraham saw a ram caught in the thicket by his horns and substituted it in place of his son (Genesis 22).

God could just as well have said, "Now I know that you understand what it is to be in covenant with Me. Everything you have (including your only son) is mine, and everything I have (including My only Son) is yours.

> Indeed, I will greatly bless you, and I will greatly multiply your seed as the stars of the heavens and as the sand which is on the seashore, and your seed shall possess the gate of their enemies. In your seed all the nations of the earth shall be blessed, because you have obeyed My voice. (Genesis 22:17)

If only we could understand that a covenant is an altar upon which the Lord and His covenant partner give themselves fully to each other. Are you willing to lay yourself on the altar and forever be a living sacrifice given to God's highest plans? Few of us truly understand the depth of commitment involved in a covenant. Doesn't this thought fly right in the face of our self-centered society? Our independence is rattled at the very thought of it, and we dread the consequence of being tied down.

The reference to this impending sacrifice of his son in Hebrews 11:17 gives us an insight into what was going through Abraham's mind as he was journeying to Moriah with Isaac.

> By faith Abraham, when he was tested, offered up Isaac, and he who had received the promises was offering up his only begotten son; it was he to whom it was said, "In Isaac your descendants shall be called." He considered that God is able to raise people even from the dead, from which He also received him back as a type.

This act of faith is also referred to in James 2:21.

> Was not Abraham our father justified by works when he offered up Isaac his son on the altar? You see that faith was working with his works, and as a result of the works, faith was perfected; and the Scripture was fulfilled which says, "And Abraham believed God, and it was reckoned to him as righteousness," and he was called the friend of God.

In biblical times two people became friends when they had cut covenant. They did not refer to the term *friend* lightly or casually. The term meant that they were in a blood pact for life. In 2 Chronicles 20:7, this reference is made: "Did You not, O our God, drive out the inhabitants of this land before Your people Israel and give it to the descendants of Abraham, Your friend forever?"

A covenant was always accompanied by blood and an oath. In Hebrews 6:13, we are told some very astounding information. It is marvelous that our God has entered into covenant with mankind! "For when God made the promise to Abraham, since He could swear by no one greater, He swore by Himself, saying, 'I will surely bless you and I will surely multiply you.'"

God Entered into Covenant with Man

God has been in covenant with His human creation from the beginning. No other religion in the world offers such a foundation of unconditional love. On His own initiative, out of the motivation of lovingkindness, God entered into covenant with man. The following words are part of the Song of Moses in Exodus 15:11: "Who is like You among the gods, O Lord? Who is like You, majestic in holiness, awesome in glory, working wonders?"

Why is Christendom not ecstatic over the kind of God we have? Why are we more complacent than exultant that He is in a covenant with us? We should be shouting this good news from the rooftops! Our God is love! He is unlike any other god! He has cut a covenant with His Son and invited us to be in covenant with Him by faith. If we open ourselves up to Him and allow the Holy Spirit to make this a reality, our lives will be utterly transformed. "Oh, the depth of the riches both of the wisdom and knowledge of God! How unsearchable are His judgments and unfathomable His ways" (Romans 11:33).

When God called Abram, He put into motion a plan to save all the people of the world. We will see that all along the trail of blood God has made covenants for the recovery of the human family from the sentence of sin and death. Through Abraham, all the families of the earth are blessed because Jesus Christ came through the lineage of Abraham. We can appropriate the promises of the God of the Covenant by faith, take hold of the scarlet cord, and make our way to eternity.

In referring to the gospel that has been handed to us, Paul says, "For in it the righteousness of God is revealed from faith to faith; as it is written, "But the righteous man shall live by faith (Romans 1:17).

Abraham and Sarah are great models of a marriage covenant lived out for the glory of God together. Their faith and obedience are praiseworthy. Because they were also in covenant with God, they accomplished the impossible and fulfilled God's purposes in their lifetime.

The curtain falls on Abraham purchasing a small burial plot for his beloved Sarah at Machpelah. He insisted on paying the full amount for this field and the cave that was on it so that it was his possession and could not revert back to the prior owner after his death. Through this transaction he could be assured that he would be buried next to Sarah someday and bequeath the site to his children, grandchildren, and future descendants. The full circle of the family covenant was complete, even in death.

CHAPTER 8

FROM FATHER TO SON TO GRANDSON

The curtain rises as the Lord appears to Isaac during a severe famine in Canaan and says,

> Do not go down to Egypt; stay in the land of which I shall tell you. Sojourn in this land and I will be with you and bless you, for to you and to your descendants I will give all these lands and I will establish the oath which I swore to your father Abraham. I will multiply your descendants as the stars of heaven, and will give your descendants all these lands; and by your descendants all the nations of the earth shall be blessed; because Abraham obeyed Me and kept My charge, My commandments, my statutes and My laws. (Genesis 26:2–5)

So Isaac obeyed his part of this covenant by living in Gerar, the land of the Philistines. Did God fulfill His side of the covenant? The Scriptures tell us that what Isaac sowed in that land, he reaped a hundredfold. As the Lord blessed him, he became rich and continued to grow richer until he was wealthy. He had possessions of herds and flocks and a great household so that the Philistines envied him.

Because of contention over the wells in that land, Isaac moved to the Valley of Gerar and then to Beersheba. Eventually Isaac made a covenant with Abimelech so that they could live in peace from that time forward. Isaac was a man of God and a man of peace. The Lord appeared to him another time and pronounced this covenant to him: "I am the God of your father Abraham; do not fear, for I am with you. I will bless you and multiply your descendants, for the sake of My servant Abraham" (Genesis 26:24).

So God gave Isaac the Abrahamic covenant to pass on to his descendants. It is important to note why the Lord made this covenant with Isaac. In Genesis 17:19, God had said to Abraham,

> Sarah your wife will bear you a son, and you shall call his name Isaac; and I will establish My covenant with him for an everlasting covenant for his descendants after him.

God always keeps His promises.

Abraham had sent his servant to his homeland in Mesopotamia to find a bride for Isaac. He did not want Isaac to choose a Canaanite wife with the possible entanglement of idol worship. The servant returned with Rebekah, a woman of God's own choosing, and Isaac loved her and married her. When Rebekah was barren for twenty years, Isaac prayed to the Lord on behalf of his wife, and the Lord answered him. Rebekah conceived twins, Esau and Jacob. When the infants seemed to struggle in her womb, the Lord said to her,

> Two nations are in your womb; and two peoples will be separated from your body; and one people shall be stronger than the other; and the older shall serve the younger. (Genesis 25:23)

Here again we can see how God's master plan is strategically put into motion. Jacob was chosen by God to be one of His key players in the ongoing covenant of salvation. Isaac and Rebekah were married for twenty years before she conceived, but the timing of the Lord was perfect. Jacob was the instrument God ordained to implement the early beginnings of the nation of Israel.

Even though Esau was the firstborn, he didn't regard his birthright blessing from his father to be something of high value. One day when he came in from the fields famished, he sold his birthright to Jacob for a pot of lentil stew that Jacob was cooking. Later when Rebekah heard that Isaac was about to bestow the birthright blessing on Esau, she and Jacob devised a plan to trick Isaac since his eyesight was dim. She brought Esau's clothes for Jacob to wear, and skins of young goats for his arms and neck, because Esau was a hairy man. In this way Isaac thought he was blessing Esau.

It is likely that Rebekah and Jacob thought that Jacob's blessing was God's will because of God's prophetic words to Rebekah, but they took it upon themselves to make it happen. The consequence of this was that Esau was enraged when he discovered what had happened and let it be known that he would kill Jacob after Isaac died.

Rebekah pleaded with Isaac to send Jacob away, using the excuse that he might marry a Canaanite woman if he stayed like Esau had. Esau had married two daughters of Heth, and they had brought grief to Isaac and Rebekah. Isaac blessed Jacob with the covenant of Abraham as he left home.

> May God Almighty bless you and make you fruitful and multiply you, that you may become a company of peoples. May He also give you the blessing of Abraham, to you and to your descendants with you, that you may possess the land of your sojournings, which God gave to Abraham. (Genesis 28:3–4)

Isaac exhorted him not to take a wife from among the daughters of Canaan. He told him to go to Paddan-aram to the house of Bethuel and take a wife from the daughters of Laban, Rebekah's brother.

So Jacob set out toward Haran, and when the sun had set, he came to a certain place. He placed a stone under his head for a pillow and lay down to sleep. He had a dream of a ladder set upon the earth, with the top reaching to heaven, and angels were ascending and descending on it. In the dream the Lord stood above the ladder and delivered the words of His covenant to Jacob.

> I am the Lord, the God of your father Abraham and the God of Isaac; the land on which you lie, I will give it to you and to your descendants. Your descendants will also be like the dust of the earth, and you will spread out to the west and to the east and to the north and to the south; and in you and in your descendants shall all the families of the earth be blessed. Behold, I am with you and will keep you wherever you go, and will bring you back to this land; for I will not leave you until I have done what I have promised you. (Genesis 28:13–16)

When Jacob awoke, He said, "Surely the Lord is in this place, and I did not know it! He was afraid and said, This is none other than the house of God, and this is the gate of heaven" (Genesis 28:17). It is possible that Jacob had not had a personal encounter with God up until this time. He erected the stone that had been under his head as a pillar and poured oil on its top. He called the place "Bethel." He also made a vow to the Lord in return for the covenant God had made with him.

> If God will be with me and will keep me on this journey that I take, and will give me food to eat and garments to wear, and I return to my father's house in safety, then the Lord will be my God. This stone which I have set up as a pillar, will be God's house, and of all that You give me I will surely give a tenth to You. (Genesis 28:20–22)

Leah and Rachel

When Jacob came to Padan-aram, he found that his uncle, Laban, had two daughters, Leah and Rachel. Jacob fell in love with Rachel and agreed with Laban to work for him for seven years for the hand of Rachel in marriage. As it turned out, when the seven years had been completed, Laban tricked Jacob into marrying Leah first by bringing her instead of Rachel into his tent at night. So Jacob worked for another seven years to take Rachel as his bride. In the course of time, Jacob fathered twelve sons and a daughter.

It seemed that Laban did everything he could to deceive and cheat Jacob in the twenty years that Jacob was there, but the covenant of the Lord with Jacob superseded any evil efforts on Laban's part. Jacob prospered and accrued great flocks of sheep and herds of cattle. He also had male servants and camels and donkeys. Finally the Lord told Jacob to return to his father's land and to his relatives. So He gathered together his wives and children, his livestock, and all that belonged to him and set out. The Lord had kept him safe and blessed him abundantly.

Name Changed to Israel

One night when Jacob was alone by the brook, Jabbok, he wrestled with a man all night. In the book of Hosea (12:4) this man is identified as an angel of the Lord, and some scholars think that the man could have been the preincarnate Jesus. When the dawn was approaching, the man touched the socket of Jacob's thigh and found the socket was dislocated. He then told Jacob to let him go, but Jacob responded by declaring that he would not let him go unless he blessed him. The man asked Jacob his name, and when Jacob answered, "Jacob," the man replied that he would no longer be "Jacob" but "Israel" because "you have striven with God and with men and have prevailed" (Genesis 32:28). Then He blessed him. When the sun rose, Jacob was limping because of his thigh.

Can you see how each of these pieces of God's historical puzzle fits together so that suddenly we begin to see the big picture? Please keep in mind that God has engineered each event and placed each chosen person at the right time and the right place to accomplish His divine purposes. He is doing the same in our present history and wants us to believe what He says and trust Him no matter what the circumstances are.

At first Jacob settled in Shechem and the land of Canaan, but because of the treachery of his sons, who went on a killing rampage in Shechem to avenge the rape of their sister, Dinah, God told Jacob to move to Bethel. Jacob realized that his company of people were now detested by the residents of the land. Another danger lurking in the land was best expressed in these words by the men of Shechem before the rape incident: "Make marriages with us. Give your daughters to us, and take our daughters for yourselves. You shall dwell with us, and the land shall be open to you. Dwell and trade in it, and get property in it" (Genesis 34:9–10). God's call to Abraham to become the father of a great nation could not have been carried out if His people had intermarried and followed the false gods of the Canaanites. It was a call to be separate.

Jacob told his household to arise and go up to Bethel with him, and he would make an altar there to God. He testified to them that God had "answered me in the day of my distress and has been with me wherever I have gone" (Genesis 35:3). He built the altar there because God had revealed Himself to Jacob there.

God appeared to Jacob as he returned from Paddan-aram and spoke the words of the covenant to him again in Genesis 35:10–12.

I am God Almighty;
be fruitful and multiply;
a nation and a company
of nations shall come from you,
and kings shall come forth from you.
The land which I gave to
Abraham and Isaac,
I will give it to you,
and I will give the land to
your descendants after you.

Joseph and His Brothers

The sons of Jacob were aware that Jacob favored Joseph, and their jealousy caused them to hate him. The Scriptures say that Jacob loved him more than his other sons because Joseph was a son of his old age and the son of Rachel. Jacob made for him a many-colored tunic, which only made matters worse. Then Joseph began telling them of dreams that he had where they were all bowing down to Him. They hated him even more for his dreams and his words.

One day Jacob sent Joseph out to his brothers, who were pasturing the flocks, to see about their welfare. When his brothers saw him, they threw him into a pit and later sold him to Ishmaelite traders who were passing by. The brothers tore Joseph's colorful coat, dipped it in goat blood, and took it to Jacob to show him that Joseph had been devoured by a wild beast. Jacob mourned his son for many days and refused to be comforted.

The Famine

At the age of seventeen Joseph had been taken to Egypt, and Potiphar, an Egyptian officer of Pharaoh, bought him from the Ishmaelites. His master saw that the Lord was with Joseph and caused all that he did to prosper in his hand. Joseph found favor in his sight and was made overseer over his house and all that he owned. He was handsome in appearance, and his master's wife enticed him. Joseph refused to succumb to her enticement and said, "How could I do this great evil and sin against God?" (Genesis 39:9). Potiphar's wife set Joseph up and lied to her husband so that Joseph was imprisoned. During his imprisonment he gained a reputation as a dream interpreter, so when Pharaoh had a perplexing dream, he called for Joseph to interpret it. Joseph related that the dreams indicated that seven good years of abundant crops were coming followed by seven years of famine. He said that the matter was determined by God and that God would soon bring it to pass. Joseph suggested that an overseer be appointed, one who would see to it that a fifth of the grain and food during the years of plenty would be stored up in the cities under Pharaoh's authority. In this way the food would be held in reserve for the seven years of famine.

Then Pharaoh said to Joseph that since God had informed him of all of this, there was no one more wise and discerning than he was. So Pharaoh appointed Joseph to rule over all of Egypt, and the only one greater than he would be Pharaoh himself. Joseph was thirty years old when he became ruler of Egypt. He went throughout the land of Egypt, gathering all the excess food in those seven years, and he stored the food in the cities. The Bible says that the grain was like the sand of the sea until he stopped measuring it, for it was beyond measure (Genesis 41:49).

After seven years of plenty the famine began. When the famine spread over all the earth, Joseph opened his storehouses, and people from Egypt as well as surrounding lands came to Egypt to buy grain.

Family Reunion

The story of Joseph is fascinating, and even the secular world has found it to be worthy of making into a musical movie titled *Joseph and the Amazing Technicolor Dreamcoat!* Yet the truth of the matter is that Almighty God was orchestrating His plan to create a nation to be His very own. He was putting all the pieces into place. God had told Abraham many years before, "Know for certain that your descendants will be strangers in a land that is not theirs (Genesis 15:13). Among those who came to Egypt to buy grain were Jacob's sons, for the famine was also severe in Canaan. Jacob sent his sons to Egypt but kept Benjamin with him to protect him from harm. When Joseph's brothers arrived in Egypt to buy grain, Joseph recognized them but disguised himself from them and spoke harshly, accusing them of being spies. Keeping Simeon hostage, he demanded that they return with their youngest brother, Benjamin. When the brothers finally returned with Benjamin, Joseph was overcome with love for his full brother, the son of his mother. In the end Joseph, with the blessing of Pharaoh, invited his father, Jacob, and the whole family to come to Egypt and settle there. Through Joseph, God saved a whole family.

The restoration of the family was emotional and heartfelt. Jacob and his twelve sons had been through deception, jealousy, anger, and guilt. When Joseph revealed himself to His brothers, they were absolutely stunned and expected just retribution for what they had done. Joseph, however, said to them,

> I am your brother, Joseph, whom you sold into Egypt. Now do not be grieved or angry with yourselves, because you sold me here, for God sent me before you to preserve life. For the famine has been in the land these two years, and there are still five years in which there will be neither plowing nor harvesting. God sent me before you to preserve a remnant in the earth, and to keep you alive by a great deliverance. Now, therefore, it was not you who sent me here, but God. (Genesis 45:4–8)

We can observe in this account that the eternal bond of love in a family was still there. The Scriptures say that when Joseph made himself known to his brothers, he wept so loudly that the Egyptians heard it and the household of Pharaoh heard of it. It says that Joseph fell on his brother Benjamin's neck and wept, and then he kissed all his brothers and wept on them. Afterwards, they talked to one another.

As we read about this amazing story of Joseph, we will immediately see the link of God's covenant with Jacob to the future covenant with Moses and the people of Israel. It is a link of 430 years! Why did God choose the country of Egypt in which to preserve and nurture His chosen people? As much as Jacob wanted to see Joseph, he struggled to leave the land that had been promised to him and his ancestors in covenant. When he sought God in prayer, this is what God said:

> "Jacob, Jacob." And he said, "Here am I." Then He said, "I am God, the God of your father. Do not be afraid to go down to Egypt, for there I will make you into a great nation. I myself will go down with you to Egypt, and I will also bring you up again, and Joseph's hand shall close your eyes." (Genesis 46:2–4)

At the beginning of this chapter we noted that God spoke to Isaac during a severe famine in Canaan and told him not to go down to Egypt but to stay in the land where he was. Now God is telling Jacob to go down to Egypt because there He would make him into a great nation. God's ways are intentional. As already mentioned, Jacob's family was vulnerable to the temptation of intermarriage and the false gods of Canaan. One of Jacob's sons, Judah, had married a Canaanite woman and had sons by her (Genesis 38:2–5), and another son, Simeon, had married a Canaanite woman and had a son by her (Genesis 46:10).

Joseph was aware of this risk for his family and arranged for them to live in a part of Egypt called Goshen, which was isolated from the rest of the country and separated from the worship of Egyptian gods. When Joseph tearfully greeted his father in Goshen and welcomed his brothers, he told them that he would notify Pharaoh that his family had arrived from Canaan. He instructed them to tell Pharaoh that they were shepherds and keepers of livestock and that they had brought their herds and flocks and all that they had with them. Joseph said that this would ensure that they could live in the land of Goshen, for "every shepherd is loathsome to the Egyptians" (Genesis 46:34).

Pharaoh let it be known to Jacob and his family that the land of Goshen was at their disposal and that they could settle in the best of the land (Genesis 47:6). In this way God took the children of Israel out of Canaan with all its temptations, so they could flourish and grow and become a great and separate nation. From this point on the nation of Israel would claim their heritage to be from Abraham, Isaac, and Jacob. Each of these patriarchs had been given the covenant directly by God.

The curtain falls as the sons of Israel carry their father, Jacob, and their little ones and their wives in the wagons that Pharaoh has sent to carry them. They take their livestock and their property, which they acquired in the land of Canaan, and they arrive in Egypt—Jacob and his descendants with him, his sons and his grandsons with him, his daughters and his granddaughters (Genesis 46:5–7).

Each son of Jacob travels in a distinct group and is responsible for his own family. When they ultimately join Joseph and his family in Egypt, the very first appearance of the twelve tribes of Israel is revealed.

CHAPTER 9

FROM HOUSE TO HOUSE

The curtain rises on a scene by the bank of the Nile River. The daughter of Pharaoh has spotted a basket among the reeds and has sent her maid to fetch it for her. When she opens it, she sees a beautiful child and is filled with compassion. She says, "This is one of the Hebrews' children." The sister of the child (whose name is Miriam) has been waiting in the distance and immediately approaches Pharaoh's daughter and asks if she should call a nurse from among the Hebrew women to nurse the child. When this question is met with an enthusiastic assent, Miriam brings to her the child's mother (whose name is Jochebed), and Pharaoh's daughter tells her to take the child away and nurse him, and she will pay her wages.

This beginning of the narrative of Moses in the Bible is a familiar one to most of us. At the outset, as we picture this baby being drawn out from the waters of the Nile, we have no idea that another spectacular saga is about to unfold in God's plan of salvation through His eternal covenant and through his families on the earth. In fact, it seems as if the family walks out on center stage in this opening act. First there is Moses in the basket, and then there is his sister, Miriam, and finally his mother, Jochebed, stretching out her arms to take her son and nurse him until he is weaned (and getting paid for it).

To refresh our memories, we need to take a quick look at the history of the children of Israel leading up to this scene by the Nile. Many years before, Joseph had been the ruler of Egypt and had brought his father, Jacob, and his whole family to Egypt because of a famine in Canaan. (This is another picture of a whole family being saved by the grace and foreknowledge of God.) Joseph said to his father and brothers,

> You shall live in the land of Goshen, and you shall be near me, you and your children and your children's children and your flocks and your herds and all that you have. There I will also provide for you, for there are still five years of famine to come, and you and your household and all that you have would be impoverished. (Genesis 4:11)

Over the years the family of Jacob grew from about seventy people to a great multitude. As long as Joseph lived, the children of Israel were treated kindly by the Egyptians, but after Joseph died, a new king began to rule. When he saw that the Israelites were numerous and growing in population, he was concerned that they soon would outnumber and overpower the Egyptians. He appointed harsh and cruel rulers over them and enslaved them. They were burdened with hard labor, building cities, making brick, and working in the fields. As a final, desperate measure to limit the number of Israelites in his land, he commanded that every son born to a Hebrew woman be cast into the Nile.

The second chapter of the book of Exodus begins with these words:

> Now Amram, a man of the house of Levi (the priestly tribe) went and took as his wife Jochebed, a daughter of Levi. And the woman became pregnant and bore a son; and when she saw that he was beautiful, she hid him three months. And when she could no longer hide him, she took for him an ark or basket made of bulrushes or papyrus, daubing it with bitumen and pitch. Then she put the child in it and laid it

among the rushes by the brink of the river Nile. (Exodus 2:1–3 AMP)

It is again apparent that the lineage of God's people is of great importance to Him. He wants to make it clear that the people of His holy covenant are connected and don't appear in Scripture as individuals out of nowhere, disconnected from their forefathers and the household of God.

Another interesting fact is that the Hebrew word for ark is *tebah*, and it is only used in the Bible twice—once when speaking of Noah's ark and then in reference to the wicker basket of bulrushes and papyrus. The basket of Moses was considered an ark. Both arks were vessels that God used to deliver His people from death for His plans and purposes. When the child grew, Jochebed brought him to Pharaoh's daughter, and he became her son. "And she named him Moses, and said, 'Because I drew him out of the water'" (Exodus 2:10).

As we proceed down the pathway of miracles, signs, and wonders in the life of Moses, we realize that his deliverance from the waters of the Nile and his placement in the palace of the princess were divine interventions from the very start! Later on we could look at Moses and say that he was qualified to lead the massive throng (two to three million) of the children of Israel out of Egypt. He understood the culture and mentality of the Egyptians and their government. He was highly educated and knowledgeable and therefore capable of controlling and managing the Israelite slaves, who had no such privilege. God could certainly have chosen him on the basis of his qualifications.

God Chose Moses and Formed His Character

Yet I believe that God chose him from birth ... just as He chooses each one of us even before we are born. It is obvious that God had

His hand and eye on Moses, carefully preserving him in the reed basket, intending that he be reared in royalty and luxury, watching his passion as he killed an Egyptian who was beating a Hebrew slave, knowing that Moses fled from Pharaoh into the land of Midian. Moses had spent forty years in the palace as a prince, and now he was spending forty years in the wilderness and desert of Midian as a shepherd. God had a work for Moses to do. All this time and through the contrast of these experiences, God was preparing, equipping, and molding Moses for this work.

In the end Moses had the character and integrity of a man of God. God Almighty, the Father in heaven, formed and developed Moses along the way to be a great leader. A few verses in Scripture give us an insight into the character of the man Moses. In the middle of the journey through the desert, an incident occurs in which Miriam and Aaron (the sister and brother of Moses) challenge his authority. They said, "Has the Lord indeed spoken only through Moses? Has he not spoken through us as well? And the Lord heard it. Now the man Moses was very humble, more than any man who was on the face of the earth" (Numbers 12:2). Isn't that a great tribute and testimony to his character, written into the Holy Scriptures forever after? This is God's answer to Miriam and Aaron: "With my servant Moses, He is faithful in all My household; with him I speak mouth to mouth" (Numbers 12:7–8).

After Moses died, it is recorded that Joshua, the son of Nun, was filled with the spirit of wisdom, for Moses had laid his hands on him, and the sons of Israel listened to him and did as the Lord had commanded Moses (Deuteronomy 34:9). So two remarkable character traits are singled out, namely humility and wisdom, but others are also included—strength, courage, and steadfast service to his God.

A Family Affair

Before we go on to consider the nature of this massive assignment given to Moses by our great God, I want to pause for a moment to give attention to Miriam and Aaron. From a young age Miriam had the confidence to approach the princess of Egypt in regard to the care for baby Moses. She will forever play an immortal part in the glorious exodus and journey in the wilderness of the children of Israel toward the Promised Land. When God miraculously delivered His people from the pursuing Egyptian Army at the Red Sea, we first learn that Miriam was a prophetess!

> Then Miriam the prophetess, Aaron's sister, took a tambourine in her hand, and all the women followed her, with tambourines and dancing. Miriam sang to them:
> Sing to the Lord,
> for he is highly exalted.
> The horse and its rider
> he has hurled into the sea.
> (Exodus 15:20–21)

This song is still sung thousands of years later in our churches and synagogues. When God presented Moses with this stupendous task of leading the nation of Israel (which had not yet been identified as a nation) out of the nation of Egypt, Moses protested. Moses said to God, "Who am I, that I should go to Pharaoh, and that I should bring the sons of Israel out of Egypt?" This was followed by, "What if they will not believe me or listen to what I say? For they may say, 'The Lord has not appeared to you.'" Then Moses said to the Lord, "Please, Lord, I have never been eloquent, neither recently nor in time past; nor since You have spoken to Your servant; for I am slow of speech and slow of tongue." God countered each of these questions, but to the last one, He asked, "Is there not your brother Aaron the Levite? I know that He speaks fluently. And moreover, behold, he is coming out to meet you; when he sees you he will be glad in his heart" (Exodus 4:14).

Aaron became the mouthpiece of Moses. God said to Moses, "He will be as a mouth for you and you will be as God to him." Aaron was also the first high priest from the tribe of Levi. He and his children and his descendants after him served in the worship of the tabernacle as long as it continued. Aaron represented the people before God and spoke for Moses when they represented God before Pharaoh. Aaron also was involved in many miracles with Moses in their long odyssey out of Egypt and across the desert.

These siblings—Moses, Aaron, or Miriam—were not sinless or perfect. Aaron made some bad choices, such as helping the Israelites make an idol of the golden calf, while Moses was on Mount Sinai. When Moses returned to the camp, he burned with anger and asked Aaron how this had come to be! Aaron replied in Exodus 32:22–24,

> Do not let the anger of my lord burn; you know the people yourself, that they are prone to evil. For they said to me, 'Make a god for us who will go before us; for this Moses, the man who brought us up from the land of Egypt, we do not know what has become of him.' I said to them, whoever has any gold, let them tear it off. So they gave it to me, and I threw it into the fire, and out came this calf.

As referred to before, Miriam and Aaron had murmured about Moses marrying a Cushite woman and wondered if the Lord spoke only through Moses and not through them as well. When the Lord heard this, He burned with anger and called the three of them before Him at the doorway of the tent. He asked them why they were not afraid to speak against His servant, Moses. When the Lord's presence had departed, Miriam was leprous, as white as snow. Aaron begged

Moses, "Do not account this sin to us, in which we have acted foolishly and sinned." So Moses cried out to the Lord, "O God, heal her I pray!" The consequence of this incident was that Miriam was shut up for seven days outside the camp, and the people did not move on until Miriam was received again (Numbers 12:1–15).

Both Moses and Aaron were implicated in the disobedience of striking the rock at Meribah. The Lord had spoken to Moses, saying, "Take the rod; and you and your brother, Aaron, assemble the congregation and *speak* to the rock before their eyes, that it may yield its water" (Numbers 20:8).

Moses and Aaron gathered the assembly before the rock. Moses said, "Listen now, you rebels; shall we bring forth water for you out of this rock?" Then Moses lifted his hand and *struck* the rock twice with his rod, and water gushed forth for the people and their animals to drink. However, the Lord said to Moses and Aaron, "Because you have not believed Me, to treat Me as holy in the sight of the sons of Israel, therefore you shall not bring this assembly into the land which I have given them" (Numbers 20:9ff).

Despite the flaws and failures of Moses, Aaron, and Miriam, the Lord chose these three siblings to lead His chosen people from slavery in Egypt through the perils of the desert to freedom in the Promised Land! Each one of them provided their own style of leadership and dovetailed each other's strengths and weaknesses. In Micah 6:4, God says to the people of Israel, "Indeed, I brought you up from the land of Egypt and ransomed you from the house of slavery. And I sent before you Moses, Aaron, and Miriam."

As we continue to follow God's heart through the Scriptures, we discover that the progression of His spiritual history and covenants are tied together with the *family* from beginning to end.

After more than four hundred years God heard their groaning, and God remembered His covenant with Abraham, Isaac, and Jacob. God took notice of the sons of Israel in their plight. When it mentions that God remembered, it doesn't mean that God forgot! God took an oath to enter into covenant with man and swore by Himself that He would fulfill all that He had promised. As He walked through the blood of the divided animals, God had said to Abram in Genesis 15:13:

> Know for certain that your descendants will be strangers in a land that is not theirs, where they will be enslaved and oppressed four hundred years. But I will judge the nation whom they will serve, and afterward they will come out with many possessions. Then in the fourth generation they will return here, for the iniquity of the Amorite is not yet complete.

The Mission of Moses

Obviously God had not forgotten His people, and now the time of deliverance was at hand. The "fullness of time" and the "iniquity of the Amorite" must have been complete. He spoke to Moses from the burning bush and said, "I am the God of your fathers, the God of Abraham, the God of Isaac, and the God of Jacob." After He identified Himself with His covenant name, He proceeded to give Moses his mission. "Therefore, come now, and I will send you to Pharaoh, so that You may bring My people, the sons of Israel, out of Egypt" (Exodus 3:10).

Some of you are familiar with Pharaoh's flip-flopping when Moses and Aaron approached him to request that he release the Hebrews from the land of Egypt. Time after time the Lord commanded Moses to tell Aaron what to speak to Pharaoh to convince him to let the sons of Israel go. Then it followed that either God would harden Pharaoh's heart or Pharaoh would harden his own heart. In this way the Lord's signs and wonders could be displayed and manifested in the land of Egypt. By severe plagues and great judgments the Egyptians would ultimately be convinced that He was the Lord and that it was He who brought out the sons of Israel from their midst.

After a series of nine horrendous plagues, such as rivers turning to blood, frogs, locusts, and hail, Pharaoh relented and said that the people of Israel could go and then soon changed his mind. The Lord told Moses that he would send a tenth and final plague and that afterward Pharaoh would finally let them go. The Lord said through Moses that at midnight He would go out in the midst of the land of Egypt and that all the firstborn in the land of Egypt would die, including the firstborn of the cattle. This is what the Lord said to Moses and Aaron:

> Tell all the congregation they shall take every man a lamb, according to the size of the family of which he is the father, a lamb for each house. And if the household is too small to consume the lamb, let him and his next door neighbor take it according to the number of persons, every man according to what each can eat shall make your count for the lamb. Your lamb shall be without blemish, a male of the first year. And you shall keep it until the fourteenth day of the same month, and the whole assembly of the congregation of Israel shall each kill his lamb in the evening. (Exodus 12:3–6 AMP)

According to instructions, the Hebrews brought their lambs to their doorsteps and killed them. As they killed their animals, they caught the blood in a basin at the foot of the doorstep. With hyssop branches dipped in blood, they sprinkled the blood on the two doorposts and on the lintel above the doorpost. The life of the sacrifice was in the blood (Leviticus 17:11). Effectively the blood covered the entire entrance to the house. The blood was like a scarlet cord draped around the perimeter of the door for the salvation of the household. Even at that ancient time we can see that the blood of the lamb was a type and shadow of the blood of Jesus, which we apply over our houses, our children, and families by faith so that the Destroyer cannot come in. The lamb had to die in the stead of the firstborn of each household. The symbolism of the sacrifice of the lamb and the shed blood over their entrances, foreshadowed the Lamb of God, who died in our stead for the forgiveness of sins. "When John saw Jesus coming to him, he said: 'Behold, the Lamb of God who takes away the sin of the world'" (John 1:29).

The Sign of the Blood: The Passover

God had said to Moses and Aaron that the blood on the entrances to the houses would be a "sign for you, and when I see the blood, I will pass over you, and no plague of death will enter your houses, when I smite the land of Egypt." God went on to say, "This day shall be for you a memorial day, and you shall keep it as a feast to the Lord; throughout your generations you shall observe it as an ordinance forever" (Exodus 12:24). This was the Lord's Passover. "For Christ, our Passover, also has been sacrificed. Therefore, let us celebrate the feast" (1 Corinthians 5:7).

God said to the Hebrews that they should observe this event as an ordinance for them and for their children.

> When you enter the land which the Lord will give you, as He has promised, you shall observe this rite. And when your children say to you, "What does this rite mean to you?" you shall say, "It is a Passover sacrifice to the Lord who passed over the houses of the sons of Israel in Egypt when He smote the Egyptians, but spared our homes." (Exodus 12:24)

The masterful hand of the Great Shepherd was manifested to the families of the Israelites as they prepared to leave Egypt behind. The father of the family was to find a lamb without spot or blemish that would be sufficient to feed his family, a lamb for a house. They were to roast and eat the entire lamb along with unleavened bread and bitter herbs. If their family was too small to eat an entire lamb, they were to include their next-door neighbors in the meal, according to the numbers of people. The Hebrews of the Exodus have given us an indelible picture of the oneness of a family united in a covenant of faith with God! It further shows the willingness we should have to extend the abundant blessings of our households of faith, love, and material possessions to those God gives to us.

The people were further instructed to have their loins girded that night, their staffs in their hands, to eat in haste, to carry the baked cakes and kneading bowls of unleavened bread bound up in their clothes on their shoulders, and to be fully prepared for the journey. This description of the preparations of the Hebrews on the night of their departure from Egypt so long ago allows us to see and understand the love and endearment that God the Father has for His families on this earth. Of all the scenarios He could have chosen to initiate for this miraculous and unforgettable deliverance of God's people, He began with their families. His final command was, "None of you shall go outside the door of his house until morning" (Exodus 12:22). What a graphic example this is of enclosing our families in the arks of our spiritual households, closing the door to the influence of the world and the devil, and keeping them under the cover of the blood of Jesus!

At midnight the Lord struck all the firstborn in the land of Egypt, and there was a great cry in Egypt, for there was no home where there was not someone dead. Pharaoh arose in the night and called for Moses and Aaron. He said, "Rise up, get out from among my people, both you and the sons of Israel" (Exodus 12:31).

The Exodus

The curtain falls as more than two million Hebrews set out on foot from Egypt with their flocks, herds, and a large number of livestock. They walk out in order like a great army, family by family and tribe by tribe. God has chosen a family of three (Moses, Aaron, and Miriam) to lead this exodus of the Hebrews from Egypt, one of the most remarkable and important historical events of all time.

Each family had a whole lamb inside of them.

CHAPTER 10

FROM HAND TO MOUTH

The Red Sea

The curtain rises as the Lord is leading the sons of Israel around by way of the wilderness to the Red Sea in a pillar of cloud by day and in a pillar of fire by night to give them light. This provision enabled them to travel both day and night and was not taken from them until they reached the Promised Land. God said, "Behold, I am going to make a covenant. Before all your people I will perform miracles which have not been produced in all the earth nor among any of the nations; and all the people among whom you live will see the working of the Lord" (Exodus 34:10). In this way God displayed His wonder-working signs and showed his faithfulness to the covenant from their first steps out into the desert.

As they neared the Red Sea, Pharaoh once again changed his mind and led his armies in hot pursuit. The pillar of cloud that had gone before them suddenly moved and went behind them so that it came between the camp of Egypt and the camp of Israel. The pillar of cloud along with the darkness of the night prevented the Israelites from being seen. Then Moses stretched out his hand over the sea, and the Lord divided the waters and swept them back on either side by a strong east wind, creating a dry path over which the Israelites could walk. Later Moses and the sons of Israel sang this verse in a song to the Lord: "In your lovingkindness you have led the people whom You have redeemed; In Your strength You have guided them to Your holy habitation" (Exodus 15:13).

At the very beginning of this journey God laid down the red carpet of His covenant to usher them into the wilderness with the words, "The Lord is the One who goes ahead of you; He will be with you. He will not fail you or forsake you. Do not fear or be dismayed" (Deuteronomy 31:8).

Maybe when they understood what a covenant was, they could learn to trust God for their every need. At this point in their deliverance God could only demonstrate His love and faithfulness to them. After the Israelites had passed through the Red Sea on the pathway prepared for them, God told Moses to stretch out his hand over the sea again so the waters would come back over the Egyptians, over their horsemen and chariots. They witnessed the seawalls rushing back to their normal state to engulf the pursuing Egyptians at daybreak. In Exodus 14:30, we read,

> Thus the Lord saved Israel that day from the hand of the Egyptians, and Israel saw the Egyptians dead on the seashore. When Israel saw the great power which the Lord had used against the Egyptians, the people feared the Lord, and they believed in the Lord and in His servant Moses.

Yet the people seemed to have trouble connecting the dots from one mighty miracle to another. They needed to understand that God is a covenant God and therefore faithful to what He promises. He had promised that He would be an enemy to their enemies and an adversary to their adversaries (Exodus 23:22). He further promised that He would deliver the inhabitants of the land into their hands and would drive them out (Exodus 23:31). One of the terms of the covenant was that when the people were approaching a battle against their enemies, a priest should come near to speak to them and say,

"Do not be fainthearted. Do not be afraid, or panic, or tremble before them, for the Lord your God is the one who goes with you, to fight for you against your enemies, to save you" (Deuteronomy 20:2). This is a covenant promise. God will defend Israel from all her enemies. This covenant is as efficacious today as it was then. God has revealed His character and integrity to us and is absolutely trustworthy. Why is it still so difficult to trust Him like the psalmist David trusted his God?

> The Lord is the defense
>   of my life;
> Whom shall I dread?
> When evildoers came
>   upon me to devour my
>   flesh,
> My adversaries and my
>   enemies, they
>   stumbled and fell.
> Though a host encamp
>   against me,
> My heart will not fear;
> Though war arise against
>   me,
> In spite of this I shall be
>   confident.
> (Psalms 27:1b–3)

God had promised that He would grant the Hebrews favor in the eyes of the Egyptians so that when it was time to leave, the Israelites would not go empty-handed. He told Moses to instruct the women to ask their neighbors or women living in their house for articles of gold and silver and clothing and put them on their sons and daughters. In that way they would plunder the Egyptians. True to His promise, the Lord had granted the people favor, and they received what they had requested. God was not advising them to steal or be deceptive. Later on in Deuteronomy 15:14, God tells His people that when they set their servants free, they should not send them away empty-handed but should give to them freely according to how the Lord has blessed them. He says, "You shall remember that you were a slave in the land of Egypt, and the Lord your God redeemed you." It appears that the word *plunder* is used to indicate a large amount, not coercion or force of any kind.

Another insight into how abundantly the Lord had cared for them is found in one of the final addresses of Moses to his people shortly before he died. He said, "I have led you forty years in the wilderness; your clothes have not worn out on you, and your sandal has not worn out on your foot ... nor did your foot swell" (Deuteronomy 8:4, 29:5). He continues to recount how God had blessed them and had been with them. They had not lacked a thing (Deuteronomy 2:7). The tender love of the Father for His people remains touching through these many ages. Yet Jesus Himself has said to us,

> Do not be worried about your life, as to what you will eat, or what you will drink, nor for your body, as to what you will put on ... Look at the birds of the air, that they do not sow, nor reap nor gather into barns, and yet your heavenly Father feeds them. Are you not worth much more than they? (Matthew 6:25, 26)

The people of Israel could now see that they were in a vast desert with sand and rock underneath their feet and barren hills and mountains rising up all around. Springs of water were few and far between. Moses led them along into the wilderness of Shur, and when they could find no water for three days, they grumbled to Moses. Finally they approached the waters of Marah, but much to their dismay, they found them to be too bitter to drink. This was a dire situation—a matter of life and death. Moses cried out to God and was told to throw a tree into the waters, and the bitter waters became sweet! The people could drink to their hearts' content, but God was teaching them a deeper lesson.

He wanted them to know that they themselves in their inner beings were bitter and sinful. When we read this story so many thousands of years later, it is easier for us to see the symbolism of the tree than it would have been for the Israelites. The cross (tree) of Christ is our salvation, and only when the cross is brought to bear on our lives can our sins be forgiven and our self-centered, old nature put to death. Our transformed lives become sweet and are drinkable to those who are drawn to us. "For the word of the cross is foolishness to those who are perishing, but to us who are being saved it is the power of God" (1 Corinthians 1:18).

God also wanted to prepare them for the covenant He was about to make with them. It was to be a two-way covenant, and He assured them that if they listened to His voice and did what was right in His sight, He would put none of the diseases on them that He put on the Egyptians, "for I, the Lord, am your Healer" (Exodus 15:26). He wanted them to realize that they would be unable to obey Him in and of themselves. It would be necessary for them to die to their independence and their idols and depend on Him alone. God was beginning to teach them who He was, His character, His love, and what it meant to be in covenant with Him.

Soon after on the fifteenth day of the second month after their departure from Egypt, the whole congregation grumbled against Moses and Aaron again. They complained that it would have been better to die by the Lord's hand in Egypt than to be brought into this wilderness to die of hunger! They recalled their life in Egypt, when they once sat by pots of meat while they ate their fill of bread. In response to this complaint the Lord told Moses that He would rain bread from heaven for them, and the people could go out and gather a day's portion every day. In the morning when the layer of dew evaporated, a fine, flaky substance lay on the surface of the ground. They asked, "What is it?" Moses told them,

> It is the bread which the Lord has given you to eat. This is what the Lord has commanded, "Gather of it every man as much as he should eat; you shall take an omer apiece according to the number of persons each of you has in his tent." (Exodus 16:15, 35).

Just as the Hebrews killed one lamb at the time of the Passover, enough for the entire family with none left over, now they gathered manna every morning, enough for each member of their family in the tent. God was teaching them to trust Him for their daily bread. The sons of Israel ate the manna for forty years. When they entered the land of Canaan, the manna ceased to fall. The words of the Lord's Prayer, "Give us this day our daily bread," have new covenantal meaning when we think of the bread that rained from heaven every day for forty years.

If we fast-forward to the Gospel of John in the New Testament, we read this: "Our fathers ate the manna in the wilderness; as it is written, 'He gave them bread out of heaven to eat.'" Jesus then said to them, "Truly, truly I say to you, it is not Moses who has given you the bread out of heaven, but it is My Father who gives you the true Bread out of heaven. For the Bread of God is that which comes down out of Heaven, and gives life to the world" (John 6:32–33).

The Lord spoke to Moses and said, "At twilight you shall eat meat, and in the morning you shall be filled with bread; and you shall know that I am the Lord your God" (Exodus 16:12). How longingly He wanted them to know Him and trust Him! In the evening quail came up and covered the camp, enough to feed hundreds of thousands of people. Aaron told the people that when the Lord gave them meat to eat in the evening and bread to eat to the full in the morning, they would also see His glory. They looked toward the wilderness in the morning and saw the glory of the Lord appearing in the cloud. In the New Testament when Jesus talked about the end times and the signs of His return, He said, "Then they will see the Son of Man coming in a cloud with power and great glory" (Luke 21:27). After all the grumbling of the Israelites, God providentially poured out His bread, His meat, and His glory on His beloved people.

As the congregation continued on their journey, they camped at Rephidim, where again there was no water. As usual, they quarreled with Moses and grumbled against him, accusing him of bringing them up from Egypt to kill them with thirst. God told Moses to take his staff in front of the people and strike the rock at Horeb so that water would come out from it and the people could drink. The Lord stood in the cloud before Moses as he struck at the rock, and water flowed forth from the rock in abundance to supply water for more than two million people as well as their cattle and livestock. The children of Israel camped in this area for more than a year, so the water must have been sufficient throughout that time period. To this day, deep furrows from the flow of water can be seen at the Rock of Horeb, with gaping holes and channels riddling the rock, caused by the bursting out and the gushing of water. As the water flowed from the rock, so did God's lovingkindness through the covenant. A reference is made to this miracle in 1 Corinthians 10:3, "They all ate the same spiritual food; and all drank the same spiritual drink, for they were drinking from a spiritual rock which followed them; and the rock was Christ."

Although we are struck by the long-suffering and benevolence of our Father for His people, we should also be struck by the sin of the people in complaining and grumbling against God. It is not difficult to make the leap from their hearts to ours in this present age. In 1 Corinthians Paul warns us that the sins of the Israelites in the desert happened and were written as examples and instructions for us so that we do not fall into dissension and grumbling. He says that "we should not grumble as some of them did, and were destroyed by the destroyer" (1 Corinthians 10:10). It is apparent that their complaining opened doors to the Enemy, and this somber truth applies to us as well. We cannot give vent to our grievances to the Lord and others without the consequence of losing our joy because we can't do both at once.

In Philippians 2:14, we are further impressed by the seriousness of this admonishment.

> Do all things without grumbling or disputing; so that you will prove yourselves to be blameless and innocent, children of God above reproach in the midst of a crooked and perverse generation, among whom you appear as lights in the world.

The spirit of this world is blatantly negative, critical, and complaining. As the Bible says in 2 Timothy 3:1–2, the people of this generation are lovers of self, ungrateful and unholy. As we turn to our God, who always keeps His promises, and thank Him for His goodness and mercy to us, our complaining will cease, and we will stand in contrast to the world.

It is imperative as parents and grandparents to teach our children that complaining is a sin. We can apply the truths that our God taught us through the trials of the Israelites in the wilderness so long ago to ourselves first and then also to our children and the next generation. What a different world it would be if our homes were havens of peace and contentment. We know that our Father in heaven is good and always keeps His promises. Certainly we should model for our children what it looks like to trust our God in every circumstance, making our requests and wants known to Him in prayer with thanksgiving! Then our families would appear as lights in a dark world. Then His everlasting covenant with us would become a visible reality.

Psalm 105:37ff sums up these remarkable covenantal acts of the Lord.

> Then He brought them out with silver and gold, and among His tribes there was not one who stumbled. Egypt was glad when they departed, for the dread of them had fallen upon them. He spread a cloud for a covering, and fire to illumine by night. They asked, and He brought quail, and satisfied them with the bread of heaven. He opened the rock and water flowed out; it ran in the dry places like a river. For He remembered His holy word with Abraham His servant; and He brought forth His people with joy, His chosen ones with a joyful shout.

Wouldn't it be a good idea for each one of us to write a psalm like this in honor of the Lord? Each of us has a story and a journey interspersed with the testing of our faith, high points of breakthrough and victory, and faithful provision day by day. We know that He has brought us forth with joy, but too often we don't pause to take account of all He has done for us and thank Him. Psalm 106 begins with these words, "Praise the Lord! Oh give thanks to the Lord, for He is good, for His lovingkindness is everlasting. Who can speak of the mighty deeds of the Lord, or can show forth all His praise?"

The banner over Psalm 105:8–10 is this:

> He has remembered His
>   covenant forever,
> The word which He
>   commanded to a
>   thousand generations,
> The covenant which He

made with Abraham,
and His oath to Isaac.
Then He confirmed it to
Jacob for a statute,
To Israel as an everlasting
covenant.

The curtain falls on the sons of Israel entering the wilderness of Sinai. This was the region where Moses had spent forty years as a shepherd and had heard the call of God from the burning bush. When Moses protested that he was not qualified to bring the Israelites out of Egypt, God replied in Exodus 3:12, "Certainly I will be with you, and this shall be the sign to you that it is I who sent you: when you have brought the people out of Egypt, you shall worship God at this mountain."

CHAPTER 11

FROM UP TO DOWN

The curtain rises on the scene of two to three million Israelites encamped around Mt. Sinai in the desert. We have just reviewed the extraordinary events leading up to this encampment, but now the questions need to be asked, "Who are they? Why are they here? Where are they going?" First of all, they are all descendants of the patriarchs—Abraham, Isaac, and Jacob. They are actually one enormous family related to one another by blood. What a multitudinous family reunion! More than four hundred years before, God had called Abraham and made a covenant with him. The covenant was with Abraham and his descendants throughout their generations for an everlasting covenant. God promised that He would multiply Abraham exceedingly, would bless him, and make of him a great nation. He also said that to his descendants He would give the land of Canaan. These people, who were encamped around Mt. Sinai, were the direct descendants of Jacob, whose name had been changed long ago to Israel by God (Genesis 35:10). It makes sense that this resultant family is referred to as the children of Israel. Our God is the creator of the Family Covenant. He uses His families and generations as conveyors of His divine covenants and purposes. As a newly birthed nation of Israel, these encamped people were fulfilling long-ago promises and prophecies in God's redemptive history. In fact, Moses says to them, "Yet on your fathers did the Lord set His affection to love them and He chose their descendants after them, even you, above all peoples!" (Deuteronomy 10:15).

When God called Moses from the burning bush, He identified Himself by His covenant name. "I am the God of your father, the God of Abraham, the God of Isaac, and the God of Jacob." He commissioned Moses to deliver the Hebrews out of Egypt, where they had been enslaved for 430 years. Even though Moses felt inadequate and reluctant at first, he obediently rose to the task with the help of his brother, Aaron. From that time on Moses walked hand in hand with God, and like Abraham, he accomplished this great assignment by faith.

Destination: Canaan

It was apparent that Moses had been taken into the Lord's confidence about what was happening there in the desert. In Psalm 25:14, we read that "the Lord confides in those who fear Him; He makes His covenant known to them." Each move that God makes with His covenant people has a purpose and is going somewhere. Moses knew that the Lord had chosen these people to be a holy nation for Himself and a kingdom of priests for the nations. This would be their new identity. They were here because God purposed to make a new blood covenant with them so that they would be reliant on Him from this day forward. The destination of this army was the land of Canaan, a land flowing with milk and honey.

Moses spent much time in the presence of God. When he descended the thunderous and smoking Mt. Sinai after he had spent forty days and forty nights with the Lord, the skin on his face shone because he had been so close to the Lord's glory and radiance. The Scriptures also recount that when Moses pitched his tent outside the camp of the Israelites, a pillar of cloud would appear and stand at the entrance to the tent. "Thus the Lord used to speak to Moses face to face, just as a man speaks to his friend" (Exodus 33:11). Moses prayed prayers like this: "If I have found favor in your sight, let me know your ways that I may know you" (Exodus 33:13).

With passion Moses worked in concert with the Lord to form these people into covenant-keepers and believers in the one true God.

God Makes a Covenant with His People

Three months after the exodus from Egypt, while the sons of Israel were camped in front of Mount Sinai, Moses went up to God. God took the initiative once again to make a covenant with His people. He told Moses what to say to the people,

> You yourselves have seen what I did to the Egyptians, and how I bore you on eagles' wings, and brought you to Myself. Now then, if you will indeed obey My voice and keep My covenant, then you shall be My own possession among all the peoples, for all the earth is mine; and you shall be to Me a kingdom of priests and a holy nation. (Exodus 19:4–5)

It is clear that something is different with the terms of this covenant when it is compared with God's unconditional covenant with Abraham. This covenant is a two-way street, a conditional covenant. Although the covenant with Abraham emphasized faith and this covenant with Moses emphasized the Law, they both were covenants of grace. In no way did the Mosaic Covenant nullify or make void the covenant God made with Abraham. Paul had this to say in Galatians 3:17:

> And this I say, that the covenant, that was confirmed before of God in Christ, the law, which was 430 years after, cannot disannul, that it should make the promise of none effect. For if the inheritance be of the law, it is no more of promise: but God gave it to Abraham by promise.

When Moses came down to tell the elders and the people what God had said, they eagerly answered, "All that the Lord has spoken we will do!" They had no idea what they were agreeing to since they had never entered into a covenant before, especially with Almighty God! Moses went up and down the mountain several times to hear the instructions of the Lord. He told Moses to consecrate the people, for on the third day He would descend on the mountain in a thick cloud. On that day the Lord came down in cloud and fire, and its smoke ascended like the smoke of a furnace in the sight of all the people. Thunder and lightning flashed, and the whole mountain shook and quaked. A prolonged blast of a trumpet that grew louder and louder came forth from the mountaintop and pulsated over the assembly. God wanted the people to hear Him speaking to Moses so that they would believe Moses and trust him implicitly as their leader.

Moses had brought the people out of the camp so that they could meet with God, and they stood at the foot of the mountain. When Moses spoke, the Lord answered him with a voice that sounded like thunder. The Lord proceeded to speak the words of the Ten Commandments. At this point the people were standing at a distance, trembling with fear. They pleaded with Moses to be a go-between. They urged him to hear the words of the Lord and interpret what he heard, and they would listen because they believed that if God spoke to them directly, they believed they would die. Moses exhorted them not to be afraid. He assured them that the Lord had come to test them so that they would remain in awe of Him and would not sin.

God Reveals His Character

God had performed mighty deeds to deliver His people from Egypt, and now He was revealing His righteous and holy character. They did not really know Him since they had absorbed the idolatrous ways of Egypt during their centuries of slavery. God desired His beloved people to share His character and develop a moral likeness to Him. This is what God means when He says to the people, "You shall be to Me a kingdom of priests and a holy nation" (Exodus 19:6), and when He also says, "For I am the Lord who brought you up from the land of Egypt to be your God; thus you shall be holy, for I am holy" (Leviticus 11:45).

Another aspect of God's character disclosed to them was that He is a jealous God. In no uncertain terms God made it known that they could not worship any other god, for His very name was "Jealous." He clearly told them that they should not make a covenant with any of the inhabitants of the lands into which they were going because they would be ensnared into worshipping their gods. God spoke these words to Moses:

> Thus you shall say to the sons of Israel, "You yourselves have seen that I have spoken to you from heaven. You shall not make other gods besides Me; gods of silver or gods of gold, you shall not make for yourselves." (Exodus 20:22)

God continued to reveal His character when He passed by in front of Moses on Mt. Sinai, proclaiming,

> The Lord, the Lord God, compassionate and gracious, slow to anger, and abounding in lovingkindness and truth; who keeps lovingkindness for thousands, who forgives iniquity, transgression and sin; yet He will by no means leave the guilty unpunished, visiting the iniquity of fathers on the children and on the grandchildren to the third and fourth generations. (Exodus 34:6–7)

Even the Law with its commands and demands was wrapped in grace.

It is important to realize that the Old Covenant unfolds and unfurls the revelation of God's character to us as well as to His Chosen of long ago. We might think that we already know all of these attributes of our God, but much of what we know has been derived from the Old Covenant. We need the Old Covenant as well as the New Covenant to complete the picture of who God is! It is the story of God's continual, ongoing, outflowing plan to restore the original destiny of mankind—that of being sons and daughters of the Creator. God's gift of covenant runs throughout and connects the Old Covenant with the New Covenant.

House Rules

The Lord gave Moses ordinances for the people that included rules and requirements about living together as a unique people of God. Just as each of our households has *house rules* and ways of living, so God was forming these people into a distinctive and identifiable *family*. They were to be a people of His own possession, and as their Father, He gave them laws and guidelines to teach them His expectations of how His covenant family should live. God had also declared that Israel would be a "kingdom of priests," holding them up as a model for all the other nations. In Exodus 4:22, the Lord says, "Israel is My son, my firstborn." As His firstborn son, God's intention for Israel was to be a light to the idolatrous nations around it. He called them out as a nation so that all the peoples around them would know that they worshipped a covenant-keeping God.

In Exodus 34:10, God said,

> Behold, I am going to make a covenant. Before all your people I will perform miracles which have not been produced in all the earth nor among any of the nations; and all the people among whom you live will see the working of the Lord, for it is a fearful thing that I am going to perform.

The Making of the Covenant

Moses recounted all the words and ordinances of the Lord to the people, and they answered just as jubilantly as before, "All the words which the Lord has spoken we will do" (Exodus 24:3). All of this was preparatory to God making a new blood covenant between Himself and the children of Israel. Moses wrote down all the words of the Lord and made a book of the covenant.

Then Moses rose early in the morning and built an altar at the foot of the mountain with twelve pillars for the twelve tribes of Israel. He sent young men of the Israelites to offer burnt offerings, and they sacrificed young bulls as peace offerings to the Lord. Moses took half of the blood and put it in basins, and the other half of the blood he sprinkled on the altar. Then he took the book of the covenant and read it in the hearing of the people. They said, "All that the Lord has spoken we will do, and we will be obedient!" In this case, their words spoke louder than their subsequent actions! They seemed unaware of what their part of the covenant would entail. As we look back on God's redemptive history, we need to understand that from the beginning of time God is continually disclosing Himself as a righteous and holy God desiring a covenant people who respond to Him with love and obedience. The Mosaic Covenant was like a mirror to His people, reflecting that they were incapable of keeping this law and should therefore become entirely reliant on Him. The Law was a teacher to turn them away from self-reliance and their own works and turn them toward the grace of God and the bloody sacrifices that were necessary to atone for sin.

So Moses took the blood and sprinkled it on the people and said, "Behold the blood of the covenant, which the Lord has made with you in accordance with all these words" (Exodus 24:8) The blood was like a scarlet cord flung out upon the people, which sealed the oath of covenant between God and Israel. Moses then went up the mountain again with Aaron, his sons, and seventy of the elders, and remarkably enough, they saw the God of Israel, and then they ate and drank. As representatives of the people, they were partaking of a covenant meal, which signified their communion of oneness with their God.

Afterward God called Moses further up the mountain to give him the Ten Commandments, which were engraved on both sides of two stone tablets by His own finger. These commandments formed a constitutional framework for the many laws and instructions that were to follow. God gave Moses detailed instructions regarding the building of an ark of the covenant, a tabernacle, and an altar, and He ended this meeting with the mandate that the sons of Israel should observe the Sabbath as a sign of the covenant throughout their generations perpetually and forever. Moses was with the Lord in the midst of the cloud on the mountain for forty days and forty nights.

The Golden Calf

While this momentous giving of the law was taking place on the mountaintop, the long absence of Moses below created an opportunity for a disaster waiting to happen. The people became impatient and restless and wondered if something had happened to Moses. They began to clamor around Aaron, and they begged him to make them a god, an idol to go before them. Aaron asked them to contribute their gold earrings and jewelry in order to fashioned them into a molten calf. The people said, "This is your god, O Israel, who brought you up from the land of Egypt" (Exodus 32:4). The narrative goes on to say that the next day the people offered burnt offerings and peace offerings on the altar Aaron had built before the golden calf, sat down to eat and drink, and then rose up to play. The words "rose up to play" composed a Hebrew expression with the connotation of sexual orgies, a common practice in idol worship.

Excuses could be made for this horrendous betrayal of the covenant so soon after it had been sworn to by oath. The people had been set free from their Egyptian stronghold with its many idols and deities for only three months and had fallen back into default the minute they didn't have a god (or a leader) they could see. They seemed unable to grasp the idea of an invisible God. The inherited nature of the Israelites was a fallen and sinful nature, unchanged since the fall of Adam and Eve in the Garden. God had performed great wonders on their behalf and was in the process of revealing Himself to this new nation, to these people whom He called His own. Maybe they didn't know Him well enough yet. Maybe they just didn't get the idea that in this conditional blood covenant the curse for disobedience was death! Rather than thinking of excuses for these people, we probably should seek the reaction of God to this apostasy.

> I said to them, "Cast away, each of you, the detestable things of his eyes, and do not defile yourselves with the idols of Egypt; I am the Lord your God." But they rebelled against Me and were not willing to listen to Me; they did not cast away the detestable things of their eyes, nor did they forsake the idols of Egypt. So I took them out of the land of Egypt and brought them into the wilderness. I gave them My statutes and informed them of My ordinances … But the house of Israel rebelled against Me in the wilderness … for their heart continually went after their idols. (Ezekiel 20:7–13, 16)

The scope and audacity of the golden calf was on a scale with the disobedience of Adam and Eve and the forbidden fruit. God's anger was certainly justifiable when He said to Moses, "I have seen this people, and behold, they are an obstinate people. Now then let Me alone, that My anger may burn against them and that I may destroy them" (Exodus 32:10) In the Book of Ezekiel God gives us further insight when He says that He would have poured out His wrath on them in Egypt when they did not forsake the idols of Egypt, but so that His Name would not be dishonored in the sight of the nations around them, He brought them into the wilderness. When they continued to rebel against Him in the wilderness, God says,

> Then I resolved to pour out my wrath on them in the wilderness, to annihilate them. But I acted for the sake of My Name, that it should not be dishonored in the sight of the nations, before whose sight I had brought them out. My eye spared them rather than destroying them, and I did not cause their annihilation in the wilderness. (Ezekiel 20:8–17)

So now we know how our Covenant God felt when His people again and again reverted to idol worship and rebelled against Him. Because Moses understood the covenant and spent so much time in God's presence, He immediately knew the enormity of the people's sin and all of its ramifications. It is amazing how God and Moses partnered together. God supervised this complex project of forming a people into His own possession among all the peoples and making them a kingdom of priests and a holy nation, and Moses was His point man on earth to carry it out.

Subsequently Moses interceded for the people before God because he understood both sides of the issue. He appealed to God about what the Egyptians would say if the Israelites were wiped off the face of the earth. His argument was that the Egyptians would ascribe to God an evil intent toward these people all along. Then Moses presented a very profound point.

> Turn from Your burning anger and change Your mind about doing harm to your people. Remember Abraham, Isaac, and Jacob, Your servants to whom You swore by Yourself, and said to them, "I will multiply your descendants as the stars of the heavens, and all this land of which I have spoken I will

give to your descendants, and they shall inherit it forever."
(Exodus 32:12–13)

Moses first presented the "what will people think" topic to the Lord.
This might not seem so convincing to us in view of what happened,
but to the Lord it was paramount to what He was doing here in
the wilderness. Israel was a firstborn son, and as such, was to be the
model for all the other nations that had witnessed the miraculous
exodus from Egypt as well as the other wonders God had performed
in their midst in the desert. This nation was destined to be a light to
a very dark and idolatrous world. They weren't shining very brightly
at this moment in God's redemptive history, but Moses wanted to
save the vision. They were a kingdom of priests.

We should be able to appreciate the God-given insight of Moses
when he reminded God of the Abrahamic Covenant, in which He
swore by Himself to multiply these descendants who were now
before them, to lead them to the land, which is the glory of all lands
(Ezekiel 20:15), and to bless all the nations of the earth through
his Seed!

I believe the Abrahamic Covenant saved the children of Israel in the
desert.

I also believe that God needed no reminding or convincing. This
discourse with Moses was for the sake of Moses, for the Lord
continually tests and teaches His anointed leaders about Himself
and His ways. Through this dialogue God knew that Moses truly
understood the sacredness and power of His covenants. From eternity
God knew that this sin of His people with the golden calf would
threaten the destiny of His chosen nation. Therefore, He had made
covenant promises to Abraham with an oath, and it is impossible
for God to lie or deny Himself. It was His loving foresight for them
and for us.

Consequences

Although God did not annihilate His people, they suffered some severe consequences for their contempt of the one true God. Moses melted down the calf and ground it to powder. He scattered it over the water of the brook that flowed down the mountain and made the sons of Israel drink it.

Moses stood at the gate of the camp and called out, "Whoever is for the Lord, come to me!" The men from the tribe of Levi immediately gathered around him. The Lord had instructed Moses that each of them should take his sword and go through the camp, from gate to gate, killing his brother, his friend, and his neighbor. The Levites obeyed the instructions, and three thousand men were slain that day. We might recoil at these harsh instructions, and wonder how our compassionate God could sanction this killing. It is important to keep in mind that the Israelites had sworn an oath to obey their God, to have no other gods before Him, and to put themselves under the curse of death for disobedience. Do those of us who are now in the New Covenant by faith in Jesus Christ react with horror at the consequence of our disobedience, which was the bloody and torturous death of our Savior? In Hebrews 9:22, we read these words, "According to the Law, one may almost say, all things are cleansed with blood, and without shedding of blood there is no forgiveness."

Later it is recorded that God struck the people with a plague because of what they did with the calf Aaron had made (Exodus 32:35). This was covenant justice.

The Covenant Renewed

God is also a God of lovingkindness. He told Moses to cut out two stone tablets like the first ones and to come up to Him on Mt. Sinai. Then God said that He was renewing the covenant with him.

Moses immediately bowed low toward the earth and worshipped. He said, "If now I have found favor in your sight, O Lord, I pray, let the Lord go along in our midst, even though the people are so obstinate, and pardon our iniquity and our sin, and take us as your own possession."

God gave him more ordinances and terms of the covenant, including the dictum that they should not worship any other god, for the Lord, whose name is Jealous, is a jealous God! Moses was there with the Lord on the mountain for forty days and forty nights again, and he came down with the words of the covenant, the Ten Commandments, written on the stone tablets. Moses did not know that the skin of his face shone because of his speaking with the Lord.

Atonement for Sin

In renewing His covenant with the Israelites, God knew that something more was needed. He appointed Moses, Aaron, and the Levites to institute ritual animal sacrifices for the atonement of sin. The law was given to show the people that they were prone to stray every step of the way, and through the daily, detailed instructions on how to carry out these sacrifices, they were reminded that this was necessary to atone for their sins. The specific sin of idolatry was dealt with again and again because the very animals that were sacred in Egypt were the ones that the Israelites were required to offer. An example of this is in Leviticus 17:7, when the Lord says, "They shall no longer sacrifice their sacrifices to the goat demons, with which they play the harlot. This shall be a permanent statute to them throughout their generations." Of course, the blood of bulls and goats couldn't really take away sin, but the Lord graciously accepted these sacrifices as coverings for sin. When a man placed his hands on the head of the offering on the altar, he knew that his sins were symbolically transmitted to the animal and that it was dying in his place. If it weren't for God's grace, he would be on that altar.

The Ongoing Sin of Idolatry

The everlasting God has not changed. He is the same yesterday, today, and forever. Just as He gave the Israelites the sacrifices of animals as coverings for their sins of idolatry, so He gives us the blood of Jesus to forgive us for our sins of idolatry. When the sons of Israel worshipped the golden calf, the Lord said that they had quickly turned aside from the way which He had commanded them, and His anger burned against them. His heart was broken again. How does He feel when we serve other gods and commit the sin of idolatry? Throughout the centuries mankind has worshipped one golden calf after another. Are we impervious to the law of love, which says that we should love the Lord, our God, with all our heart, with all our soul, and with all our mind? Are we deceived into thinking that we can love Him and our idols at the same time without the consequence of grieving Him? Jesus said that we cannot serve two masters, for either we will hate the one and love the other or be devoted to one and despise the other. He said we cannot serve God and Mammon. (Mammon is the money, wealth, materialism, and greed in this world.) The Bible goes on to say that the Pharisees, who were lovers of money, were listening to all these things and were scoffing at Him. Jesus addressed them by saying, "You are those who justify yourselves in the sight of men, but God knows your hearts; for that which is highly esteemed among men is detestable in the sight of God" (Luke 16:14, 15). Sometimes when modern-day Christians are confronted with this Scripture, they immediately justify themselves and insist that God has blessed them with many riches that they intend to share with others. They say that they are merely taking their places in an affluent society. Who are we to judge? Proverbs 21:2 pinpoints this issue with these words, "Every man's way is right in his own eyes, but the Lord weighs the hearts."

What do we do with the following powerful passage:

> Do not love the world nor the things in the world. If anyone loves the world, the love of the Father is not in him. For all that is in the world, the lust of the flesh and the lust of the eyes and the boastful pride of life, is not from the Father, but is from the world. (1 John 2:15)

What do we do with this? Usually we deny that this incriminating truth could apply to us, and we certainly deny that we have engaged in idolatry.

Jesus also said that "we should not store up for ourselves treasures on earth, where moth and rust destroy, and where thieves break in and steal, but store up treasures in heaven; for where our treasure is, there our hearts will be also" (Matthew 6:19–21). The underlying meaning of this statement of Jesus is interpreted further when He admonishes the rich, young ruler. "If you wish to be perfect, go and sell your possessions and give to the poor, and you will have treasure in heaven; and come, follow Me." When the ruler heard this, he became dejected and sad, for he was very wealthy (Luke 18:22–23). Statements like this are not what our old natures like to hear.

The Law as Our Tutor

The Ten Commandments served the purpose of convincing the people that they could never obey them completely. In the Book of Romans, Paul says, "For no person will be justified in His sight by observing the works prescribed by the Law. For the real function of the Law is to make men recognize and be conscious of sin" (Romans 3:20 AMP). And the Book of James says that if we keep the whole law and yet stumble in one point, we are guilty of all (James 2:10). Despite this truth and the revelations of our Lord throughout the centuries to convince mankind that we can neither fulfill the Law nor be justified by it, why is it still an issue? It is stated so clearly in Galatians 2:16, "A man is not justified by the works of the Law, but through faith in Christ Jesus."

The sacrifices were a gift of grace to the nation of Israel, but they also prefigured and pointed to the coming of Christ. "Therefore, the Law has become our tutor to lead us to Christ, so that we may be justified by faith" (Galatians 3:24).

The Israelites remained at Mt. Sinai for about a year, while God went through the process of renewing the covenant and training the Levites in their duties of the priesthood. God gave to Moses, and Moses gave to Aaron the many new rituals, laws, and ordinances to be carried out in the tabernacle.

Complaining Again

Finally the new nation set out from Mt. Sinai, with the ark of the covenant of the Lord going before them to seek out a resting place. The cloud of the Lord appeared over them when they set out from camp. After a three-day journey the Israelites were overcome again by a spirit of complaining, and the Lord heard it. His anger blazed, and His fire began to burn among them on the outskirts of the camp. Moses interceded when the people cried out to him, and the fires subsided.

God had heard the sons of Israel weeping again, and these were the words that came out of their mouths:

> Who will give us meat to eat? We remember the fish we used to eat free in Egypt, the cucumbers and the melons and the leeks and the onions and garlic, but now our appetite is gone, there is nothing at all to look at except this manna. (Numbers 11:4–6)

As a result of this recurrent crisis, God appointed seventy elders to help Moses with the burden of the people. The Lord also supplied meat for them by bringing quail from the sea. However, because of His anger, He also struck them with a severe plague because they had rejected Him by saying, "Why did we ever leave Egypt? We were well-off in Egypt" (Numbers 11:18, 20).

The curtain falls on the Israelites encamped in the wilderness of Paran not far from the border of Canaan. The Lord told Moses to send out spies, each one a leader of their fathers' tribes, to spy out the land of Canaan, which the Lord had promised to give them. It appeared that the mission of Moses to bring God's chosen people to the Promised Land was about to be accomplished.

CHAPTER 12

FROM ONE TO ANOTHER

The curtain rises on Moses as he selects a leader from each tribe of Israel to go up into the hill country and search out the land of Canaan. The time was at hand for the children of Israel to cross over the Jordan River and claim their inheritance for themselves, for their children, and for all generations to come. Moses directed them to come back with a report of which way they should go up and what the cities were like that they would enter. If they found trees and vineyards, he wanted them to bring back some of the grapes since it was the time of the first ripe grapes. They were also advised to check out the people they would be facing. Were they strong or weak? Were they few or many?

Moses must have breathed a sigh of relief when he had brought the people this close to the divine destination. It had not been an easy endeavor, but as Moses had worked closely with God in covenant partnership, he knew that God would complete what He had initiated and deliver the land into their possession. The spies returned at the end of forty days to report to Moses and Aaron and the assembly at Kadesh. Two men carried a pole with a single enormous cluster of grapes from Canaan along with pomegranates and figs. They admitted that the land did indeed flow with milk and honey just as the Lord had said, and this was the fruit of the land. They went on to say, however, that the Israelites could not possibly go up against the people of Canaan because they were too strong for them. They were men of great size, and the spies felt like grasshoppers in their sight. They lived in large fortified cities. Only Caleb and Joshua gave a good report and said, "We should by all means go up and take possession of it, for we will surely overcome it."

One of God's covenant promises to His people had been that He would be an enemy to their enemies and an adversary to their adversaries. He had promised that "I am going to send an angel before you and bring you into the land of the Amorites, the Hittites, the Perizzites, the Canaanites, the Hivites and the Jebusites; and I will completely destroy them" (Exodus 23:20–23) God had promised to the sons of Israel that He would bring them to the land that He swore to give to Abraham, Isaac, and Jacob, and that He would give it to them for a nation. Ten of the spies seemed to completely ignore, forget, or disbelieve these promises.

Another Forty Years

The sons of Israel wept that night and grumbled against Moses and Aaron. They cried,

> Would that we had died in the land of Egypt! Or would that we had died in the wilderness! Why is the Lord bringing us into this land to fall by the sword? Our wives and little ones will become plunder ... Let's appoint a leader and return to Egypt. (Numbers 14:2–4)

Can you believe it? God's reaction and reply to this was, "As I live, just as you have spoken in My hearing, so I will surely do to you; your corpses will fall in this wilderness" (Numbers 14:28-29). Those who had grumbled against the Lord and who were twenty years and older would not enter the land that the Lord had intended to give them. Their children (who were part of the family covenant) would be brought in and would receive the land that this generation had rejected. The grumbling Israelites were consigned to wandering in the wilderness for forty more years—one year for each day the spies spent in the Promised Land.

Two of the spies, Caleb and Joshua, had given a good report. They had assured their people that the land was an exceedingly good land that was flowing with milk and honey. They appealed to them not to rebel against the Lord and not to fear the people. They declared their belief that the Lord had removed His protection from the people in the land they were about to enter and would be with them. Yet despite these declarations of faith, the Israelites were ready to stone Caleb and Joshua! In the midst of this dissension, an amazing thing happened. "Then the glory of the Lord appeared in the tent of meeting to all the sons of Israel" (Numbers 14:10).

The lovingkindness of the Covenant God is astonishing, especially when He had made a conditional covenant with His people. At times like this His love must have emanated from the everlasting oath He had made to their forefathers. He was faithful even when they were unfaithful.

Because Moses knew the Lord so intimately, he understood the reaction that is recorded in Hebrews 3:17. "And with whom was He angry for forty years? Was it not with those who sinned, whose bodies fell in the wilderness? So we see that they were not able to enter because of unbelief." The Lord asked, "How long will this people spurn Me? And how long will they not believe in Me, despite all the signs which I have performed in their midst?" (Numbers 14:11). God threatened to dispossess them, but Moses again interceded on behalf of the people. The Lord relented but instructed Moses to set out the following day and lead the Israelites back out to the wilderness by the way of the Red Sea. It is not difficult to imagine how Moses felt when the consummation of his assignment had been within his grasp, and now it had been snatched away for forty more years!

God Himself had been willing to suspend His eternal purpose for the Israelites until a later time. He had brought them forth from Egypt to become His chosen people, and now He desired to carry them into the land He had promised to give them so that they would become His chosen nation. In the process of leading them He continually revealed Himself to them (and to us) so that their eyes would be opened to see Him and to know Him and His ways. Since the time of Sinai God had revealed His character through the Mosaic Covenant and the Ten Commandments to show them how much He loved them and desired to protect them from the inherent sin within themselves and others. In His mercy He had established the ritual of daily animal sacrifices for the atonement of the sins of the people and offered forgiveness through their repentance.

God longed to have His people open their hearts to the revelation that they were utterly incapable of obeying the law and walking in holiness with Him. They needed Him desperately, as do we. Yet when Moses read the Book of the Covenant to the people, they eagerly answered that they would do all that the Lord had spoken! They were clueless as to their weakness and need for Him. The underlying sin of Adam and Eve cropped up again there in the desert.

Leaning on Her Beloved

They opted to go their own way and walk independently of Him. In the Song of Solomon 8:5 the question is asked, "Who is this coming up from the wilderness, leaning on her Beloved?" It is so easy to judge the Israelites for not leaning on their Beloved, but how are we doing in this generation? Our faith may seem secure until we face a serious crisis, such as a bad health report, a financial failure, or an important decision, and then we are tempted to scramble for the many avenues of help that our minds and the world have to offer. In many ways we are self-sufficient. Do we choose to base our trust on circumstances, or do we lean heavily on our Beloved? The Israelites were intimidated by the reports of the spies and crumbled under the fear that was evoked and the unbelief that arose within themselves. Did you notice that they immediately resorted to their own thinking and problem-solving and said to one another, "Let us appoint a leader and return to Egypt"?

Had the sons of Israel ever really encountered the Lord? Did they know Him? Remember when Moses brought the people out of the camp to meet God at Sinai around the foot of the mountain? When the people heard the thunder and the sound of the trumpet and saw the lightning flashes and smoke, they trembled and stood at a distance. They implored Moses to speak to them himself because if the Lord spoke to them, they would die. Moses told the people not to be afraid, for the Lord was testing them so that reverence of Him would remain with them and they would not sin. They were not willing to draw near and stood back as Moses approached the thick cloud where God was. As we look down the corridors of time and remember all the revelations and illuminations of God's ways that He has disclosed to us, we certainly should understand Him and know His heart. The truth is that we still may not have encountered *Him*.

In the storyline that God has mapped out for all creation, we can gasp at His incredible love for all mankind and His desire to draw all men unto Himself. We know this because He had announced to Abraham in that ancient time that all the families of the earth would be blessed through him (Genesis 12:4).

In the case of the Israelites, He continually poured out His lovingkindness and faithfulness in delivering them from slavery in Egypt as well as performing miracles and marvels all along the way. As Moses said when He was reviewing the journey of the people through the desert,

> The Lord your God carried you, just as a man carries his son, in all the way which you have walked until you came to this place. But for all this, you did not trust the Lord your God. (Deuteronomy 1:31)

God reveals Himself to us as we read and study the covenants by which He has chosen to interact with mankind—from creation to Adam and Eve and onward. It is like His résumé. After we have read the biblical history of God's dealings with man, we know for certain that His love for us is everlasting, and all that we need to do is receive His love and trust Him to do what He has said He will do. Ironically we have witnessed so much more evidence of His lovingkindness and faithfulness than the Israelites did as they journeyed in the desert (like the gift of sending His Son) "and yet for all this, we sometimes do not trust the Lord our God."

Although the heart of Moses must have been heavy as he and the millions of Israelites turned toward the wilderness again by way of the Red Sea, perhaps he was comforted by the fact that his supplication to the Lord had prevented the people from being wiped out completely. His plea had been that the other nations that had heard of the Lord's fame would say that the Lord could not bring His people into the land He had promised them by oath, and therefore, He slaughtered them in the wilderness (Numbers 14:15, 16). One of the constituents of the covenant was that the nation of Israel would be a firstborn son to the Jews and a light to the Gentiles. Although God was true to His covenant of mercy and did not wipe out His people, He also was true to His justice. The men who had spied out the land and had brought back a very bad report, causing the people to grumble, died by a plague before the Lord. Out of the twelve spies, only Joshua and Caleb remained alive.

The Failure of the First Generation to Pass on a Righteous Heritage

Through many plights and perils, the sons of Israel wandered in the desert for forty years. Those who had rejected the land the Lord had given them died in the wilderness, and none were alive when the people once again convened at the border of the River Jordan. It is interesting to note that the sons of those who had grumbled and disbelieved were sentenced to be shepherds in the wilderness for forty years, suffering for the sins of their parents. I wonder what kind of parenting that first generation of Israelites did in preparing the next generation to enter and live in the Promised Land? Since their parents had learned their lessons the hard way, wouldn't they have been passionate about modeling and teaching their offspring the importance of obeying the Ten Commandments and the laws and upholding the righteous ways of the God of Abraham, Isaac, and Jacob? Since history is passed on from generation to generation, it would have been imperative to warn them about the sins of complaining, idolatry, immorality, and unbelief. A top priority for parents should be to pass down to their children what they have learned about God and share their insights and experiences as they have walked along life's path with Him. This is what the Family Covenant is all about. Yet the opposite is often true. For example, in Psalm 106:6, we read these words, "We have sinned like our fathers, we have committed iniquity, we have behaved wickedly. Our fathers in Egypt did not understand Your wonders; they did not remember your abundant kindnesses." Under the Family Covenant, we need to understand the wonders of God and remember His abundant kindnesses so that our children can inherit our knowledge and our testimonies. In Psalm 106:24, we are reminded of the first generation's ultimate sin of unbelief.

> Then they despised the pleasant land; they did not believe in His word, but grumbled in their tents; they did not listen to

the voice of the Lord. Therefore He swore to them that He would cast them down in the wilderness.

These parents had ample time to prepare their children for their long-awaited inheritance of the land of Canaan. Their daily words should have fallen like the life-giving manna on their families in the desert, filling them with descriptions of the faithful and unfailing love of God and the righteousness of His character. What parent wouldn't warn their children of the same pitfalls and dire consequences that they were even then experiencing, if they hardened their hearts and rebelled against their God? Over and over again they had learned that God would not tolerate the worship of idols and the immorality that accompanied such worship because He was a jealous God and loved them! Having been humbled, it would have been a no-brainer to teach their children that they are not able to obey the Lord at all times, and the ritual of daily animal sacrifices was available to them, as they repented and received forgiveness. The history of the Jewish people would have been different if this first generation had held up the scarlet cord of atonement as a legacy to the second generation. What an opportunity these grandparents and parents had! As a recompense to their God, they could have passed on an opposite spirit to their children and grandchildren instead of the one they had displayed!

When we finish our work on this earth and leave this life, what could be more important than having laid the foundations of faith and righteousness upon which our family can build and live their lives?

A Tragic Occurrence

Just as this second generation of Israelites was nearing their destination again, a disastrous thing happened in the plains of Moab. The prince of Moab, Balak, had hired a prophet named Balaam to curse the fledgling nation of Israel because he viewed them as a threat. Balaam had failed four times to curse the nation because of the protection of the Lord, so he advised the Moabites to invite the sons of Israel to join their daughters and cult prostitutes in idolatrous service to Baal-Peor. The Israelites ate things sacrificed to their idols, bowed down to their gods, and fell into perverse immorality and idolatry at Moab, joining themselves to Baal-Peor (Numbers 25:2). It was déjà vu to the sin of the previous generation, which had worshipped the golden calf at Sinai.

It is so easy to gloss over historical facts of long ago like the sin of the Israelites at Baal-Peor and relegate them in our minds to that time and place. After all, it is just like reading of the atrocities of mankind in ancient wars and uncivilized, archaic cultures and saying that they have nothing to do with us! We don't bow down to idols and engage in sexual revelries as a form of worship to them in America, do we? In studying the covenants in the Bible, however, with the recurrent warnings to the children of Israel to make no covenant with the inhabitants of the land, to not allow themselves to be ensnared with their idols, to tear down their altars, smash their sacred pillars, and cut down their Asherim so that they would not worship any other god, we are reminded of the verse in the New Testament that refers to this specific time in the remote past. It is found in 1 Corinthians 10:10, "Now these things happened to them as an example, and they were written for our instruction, upon whom the ends of the ages have come." It is imperative that we receive these instructions to our hearts, for that is the reason they were recorded. It is important for us to remember what happened at Baal-Peor.

If we aren't convinced by the many references to this incident in Scripture (Psalms 106:28–30; Micah 6:5) that this isn't just a recording of something long past with no relevance to us, we may leap into the future to the words of Jesus in Revelation 2:12–14, addressed to the church in Pergamum.

> The One who has the sharp two-edged sword says this: But I have a few things against you, because you have there some who hold the teaching of Balaam, who kept teaching Balak to put a stumbling block before the sons of Israel, to eat things sacrificed to idols and to commit acts of immorality.

Another New Testament verse points out the relevancy of these Scriptures to us today.

> For the word of God is living and active and sharper than any two-edged sword, and piercing as far as the division of soul and spirit, of both joints and marrow, and able to judge the thoughts and intentions of the heart. (Hebrews 4:12)

Nothing is very different now from the way it was at Baal-Peor. God is the same. He never changes. The basic nature of mankind hasn't changed either. We need to be reminded that if we don't know God or revert to our old way of thinking before we knew God, we are prone to choose the lusts of our flesh. The Word of God hasn't changed, and it is living and active and sharper than any two-edged sword. This is the difference between secular history and the spiritual history recorded in the Bible. Spiritual history is written for our instruction. It is applicable and is sharp enough to penetrate our hearts and spirits. It is as powerful as it was at Sinai and on the plains of Moab.

The influence of the world hasn't changed, remaining as deceptive and enticing as the serpent in the garden. This is exactly why God warned the Israelites over and over again to utterly annihilate the idolatrous nations they were going to overtake. God told them to make no covenant with them and to show them no compassion. He told them not to intermarry or interchange their sons and daughters because those nations would turn their sons and daughters away from God to worship other gods and ensnare them into immorality. The same warnings are given to us today in 2 Corinthians 6:14.

> Do not be bound together with unbelievers; for what partnership have righteousness and lawlessness, or what fellowship has light and darkness? Or what harmony has Christ with Belial, or what has a believer in common with an unbeliever? Or what agreement has the temple of God with idols? For we are the temple of the living God, just as God said,
>
> "I will dwell in them and walk among them;
> and I will be their God,
> and they shall be my people;
> therefore, come out
> from their midst and be
> separate, says the Lord.
> And do not touch what is unclean;
> and I will welcome you,
> and I will be a father to you,
> and you shall be sons
> and daughters to Me,
> says the Lord Almighty."

This is the covenant in a nutshell! This is our covenant relationship with our God. Were our predecessors successful in preparing us for this relationship with God? Is it too great a thing for God to ask us to come out from the midst of the world and be separate from the spirit and sin of this world? Now we have this opportunity to prepare this next generation to live in righteousness by teaching them to be dependent on the Father all the time, to walk in His ways, and to lovingly warn them not to even touch what is unclean. Are we showing them this by our example and teaching them by our words? When the second generation of Israelites was preparing to cross the

Jordan and enter the land of their inheritance, Moses spoke these words to them in Deuteronomy 6:4–9:

> Hear, O Israel! The Lord is our God, the Lord is one! You shall love the Lord your God with all your heart and with all your soul and with all your might. These words, which I am commanding you today, shall be on your heart. You shall teach them diligently to your sons and shall talk of them when you sit in your house and when you walk by the way and when you lie down and when you rise up. You shall bind them as a sign on your hand and they shall be as frontals on your forehead. You shall write them on your doorposts of your house and on your gates.

When Moses addressed the people for the last time before his imminent death and before they entered Canaan, he first turned their attention to God and what He had done for them. It is not hard to imagine how Moses felt after the reprehensible fall into idolatry and immorality that had just taken place at Baal-Peor, and his plea to them to turn their attention to God is very moving.

> Has any people heard the voice of God speaking in the midst of the fire, as you have heard it, and survived? Or has a god tried to go to take for himself a nation from within another nation by trials, by signs and wonders and by war and by a mighty hand and by an outstretched arm and by great terrors, as the Lord your God did for you in Egypt before your eyes? To you it was shown that you might know that the Lord, He is God; there is no other besides Him.

Just as God intended to reveal His character and heart to the children of Israel, He also wanted to test them and know what was in their hearts. He had received His answer soon enough. Toward the end of the Book of Deuteronomy before the people entered the land of

Canaan, the Lord said to Moses, "This people will arise and play the harlot with the strange gods of the land into the midst of which they are going, and will forsake Me and break My covenant which I have made with them." Later He said, "I know their intent which they are developing today, before I have brought them into the land which I swore" (Deuteronomy 31:16, 21).

Another Covenant

As crucial as it was for the first generation to pass down their heritage of faith to the second generation, it was also essential for the second generation to embrace the covenant of God as their own. For this reason Moses made another covenant with the Israelites at Moab. The Lord instructed Moses to make this further covenant with the Israelites forty years later because this generation had been below the age of twenty when the first covenant was made at Sinai. Deuteronomy 29 begins by saying, "These are the words of the covenant which the Lord commanded Moses to make with the sons of Israel in the land of Moab, besides the covenant which He had made with them at Horeb." He gathered his people together, including the chiefs, tribes, elders, officers, the wives, and little ones, and encouraged them to enter into the covenant with the Lord, their God, so that He would establish them today as His people and would be their God just as He swore to their fathers, Abraham, Isaac, and Jacob. Moses added that this covenant and oath were for all of them who stood there that day as well as those who were not there that day. Since this generation of Israelite males had not been circumcised along the way, Joshua had them circumcised a few days later after they had crossed the Jordan into the Promised Land. They underwent circumcision and observed the Passover before they attacked Jericho. These acts were the sign and seal of the covenant.

God had prophesied through Moses that when the people entered the land and had children and children's children, they would act corruptly and make idols and do evil in the sight of the Lord. As a consequence, the Lord would scatter them among the nations to serve gods of wood and stone. At the same time He assured them that if they would seek the Lord, even in those extenuating circumstances, He would not fail them or destroy them but would remember the covenant with their fathers, which He swore to them. It was also prophesied that when distress came upon them in the latter days, they would return to the Lord and listen to His voice (Deuteronomy 4:25–31).

Life or Death

The Book of Deuteronomy is steeped with history, the redemptive plan of God for mankind, and His holiness and righteousness alongside the rebellion and disobedience of His people. The pages also overflow with deep spiritual wisdom and the passion of the heart of the Father. Despite all this, the abundance of words tumble out like the letters of a Scrabble game and spell out this simple choice—*life* or *death*. Moses presents this choice to the people of Israel (and to us.)

> I call heaven and earth to witness against you today, that I have set before you life and death, the blessing and the curse. So choose life in order that you may live, you and your descendants, by loving the Lord your God, by obeying His voice, and by holding fast to Him; for this is your life and the length of your days. (Deuteronomy 30:19–20)

This simple choice had also been clearly presented to Adam and Eve in the Garden. They had been warned by God that if they ate from the Tree of the Knowledge of Good and Evil, they would surely die (spiritually). They chose the path of disobedience and death. Why? I believe the answer is that they desired "to be like God" and declare their independence. The hurdle, when we are confronted with this choice, is our innate quest for independence and self-rule.

The Lord was concerned about His Chosen People when they settled in the land flowing with milk and honey. He voices this concern in Deuteronomy 8:12.

> When you have eaten and are satisfied, and have built good houses and lived in them, and when your herds and your flocks multiply, and your silver and gold multiply, and all that you have multiplies, then your heart will become proud and you will forget the Lord your God who brought you out from the land of Egypt. You may say in your heart, "My power and the strength of my hand made me this wealth." But you shall remember the Lord your God, for it is He who is giving you power to make wealth, that He may confirm His covenant which He swore to your fathers, as it is this day. (Deuteronomy 8:17–18)

The Song of Moses

As the final days of the life of Moses approached, the Lord appeared in a pillar of cloud at the doorway of the tent of meeting, and Moses and Aaron presented themselves. God proceeded to tell Moses to compose a song and teach it to the sons of Israel. In fact, he was told to put the words in their very mouths so that the song would be a witness for God against the sons of Israel. The Lord explained that when the people became prosperous in the land, they would turn to other gods and serve them and reject God and break His covenant. He predicted that when many evils and distresses had come upon the people because of their apathy and apostasy, this song would testify before them as a witness, for it would not be forgotten from the lips of their descendants! So as one of his last assignments, Moses composed this song, which is found in Deuteronomy 32, and taught it to the people of Israel. Here are a few of the verses:

Remember the days of
    old,
Consider the years of all
    generations.
Ask your father, and he
    will inform you,
Your elders, and they will
    tell you. (verse 7)

But Jeshurun grew fat
    and kicked—
You are grown fat, thick,
    and sleek—
Then he forsook God
    who made him,
And scorned the Rock of
    his salvation.
They made Him jealous
    with strange gods;
With abominations they
    provoked Him to anger.
They sacrificed to
    demons who were not
    God,
To gods whom they have
    not known,
New gods who came
    lately,
Whom your fathers did
    not dread.
You neglected the Rock
    who begot you,
And forgot the God who
    gave you birth. (verses 15–18)

Usually we consider the covenant of God to be adhered to by the older generation and passed on to the next generation. But here in Deuteronomy God asks Moses to compose a song that will be inscribed on the lips of the descendants of the people so that they can act as a witness against the older generation when they break the covenant! He told him to put this song into the very mouths of their children. The covenant works both ways.

This odyssey of Moses and the people of Israel is a powerful depiction of God's covenant plan for salvation. The all-knowing Creator knew from the beginning that man would choose independence and rebellion over dependency on Him and obedience. Mankind just doesn't have a heart for God. As God implemented His plan along the way, He used His Holy Covenants to pave the way and utilized families and generations to accomplish His purposes.

The People of God

As Moses summarizes this whole Exodus and wilderness adventure in the Book of Deuteronomy, we are able to empathize with His frustrations and at the same time face the reality of the sins of our fallen natures. It was a miracle that the Israelites ever got out of that desert! Yet despite all the failures and setbacks, Moses accomplished the assignment God had given Him. We can remember how inadequate he felt at first to commit to this enormous task and how faithful he was to fulfill the commands of the Lord. In the end he had brought the people, who were not a people, out of slavery in Egypt and had formed them into a people. "The Lord has taken you and brought you out of the iron furnace, from Egypt, to be a people for His own possession, as today" (Deuteronomy 4:20).

These people of God were about to cross over the Jordan River to claim their inheritance of the Promised Land, and by so doing, they would become the nation of God. In 1 Peter 2:9, it says, "But you are a chosen race, a royal priesthood, a holy nation, a people for God's own possession, so that you may proclaim the excellencies of Him who has called you out of darkness into His marvelous light; for you once were not a people, but now you are the people of God." Our Father had been faithful to His covenant promises.

The Death of Moses

The curtain falls as Moses goes up from the plains of Moab to Mount Nebo to the top of Pisgah, which is across from Jericho, and sees a panoramic view of the Promised Land, which God swore to Abraham, Isaac, and Jacob to give to their descendants. Moses, the great servant of the Lord, died there, and God buried him there in the valley of the land of Moab.

The Bible says that since that time no prophet has risen in Israel like Moses, whom the Lord knew face-to-face.

CHAPTER 13

FROM THE DESERT TO THE HOLY LAND

The curtain rises as Joshua, the son of Nun, is leading the people of Israel to the banks of the Jordan River. The mantle of leadership was passed on to Joshua when Moses died. The Lord had spoken to Joshua and said,

> Moses My servant is dead; now therefore arise, cross this Jordan, you and all this people, to the land which I am giving to them, to the sons of Israel. Every place on which the sole of your foot treads, I have given it to you, just as I spoke to Moses. (Joshua 1:1–3)

In the Book of Numbers, the Lord referred to Joshua as "a man in whom is the Spirit" and told Moses to lay his hand on him and commission him, standing before Eleazar, the priest, and all the congregation. God also said, "You shall put some of your authority on him, in order that all the congregation of the sons of Israel may obey him" (Numbers 27:18).

This was an important step in the continuity of the leadership of Israel, and yet it was a very smooth transition, considering the loss of such a beloved and faithful leader, Moses. One short scriptural statement that carries poignant meaning in regard to the character of Joshua appears way back in Exodus. Moses used to set up his tent in the desert quite a distance from the camp. When Moses went out to the tent, the pillar of cloud would descend, and the Lord would speak to Moses face-to-face. Then all the people would rise and stand at the entrance to their tents and worship. "When Moses returned to the camp, his servant, Joshua, the son of Nun, a young man, would not depart from the tent" (Exodus 33:11).

Joshua had experienced the hardships of slavery in Egypt and also witnessed the miracles of the plagues and the parting of the Red Sea. As a young man, he had shown himself to be a warrior when he led the Israelites to victory over the Amalekites. He alone had accompanied Moses up the mountain at Sinai when the tablets of the Ten Commandments were given. He and Caleb, who was of the tribe of Judah, were the only two spies who returned from the land of Canaan with a good report and were willing to believe God and take immediate possession of the land. Because of his faith and obedience, he was not condemned to die in the wilderness along with his unbelieving generation. Joshua had quite a résumé!

Above all, the most important qualification for the task at hand was that God had chosen him just as He had chosen Noah, Abraham, Aaron, and Moses. God had chosen him to complete the work of Moses by leading Israel into the Promised Land, conquering their enemies, dividing the land among the twelve tribes, and reminding the people to be obedient to the covenant of the Lord. God had chosen him as His representative to fulfill the long-ago promise to Abraham and his descendants to give them a nation to call their own.

As Joshua began this venture to conquer the land of Canaan, he first sent two spies across the Jordan River to scout out the territory, especially Jericho. As the spies came to the city, they lodged at a house of a harlot that was built into the wall of the city. What happened next is a graphic and unforgettable picture of the family covenant, which God has imprinted on the hearts of man. The harlot, whose name was Rahab, heard that the king of Jericho was sending his soldiers to bring out the men from Israel who were staying with her, so she hid them on her roof under the stalks of flax that she had laid in order. She admitted to the soldiers that some men had come to her but said that she hadn't known where they were from and that they had left when it was time to shut the gate at dark. She didn't know where they went. She urged them to pursue the men quickly.

After the king's men left, Rahab went up to the men of Israel on the roof. She told them that she knew that the Lord had given them the land. The terror of them had fallen on all the inhabitants of the land because they had heard how the Lord had parted the waters of the Red Sea when they had come out Egypt. They had also heard that the Israelites had completely destroyed the two kings of the Amorites east of the Jordan. She then declared this statement of faith: "When we heard of it, our hearts melted, and everyone's courage failed because of you, for the Lord your God is God in heaven above and on the earth below" (Joshua 2:8–11).

We are reminded that Israel was never intended to be the only recipient of God's blessings. God had promised to bless all people through that nation (Genesis 12:1–3). Remember when God said, "The Egyptians shall know that I am the Lord, when I stretch out My hand on Egypt and bring out the sons of Israel from their midst" (Exodus 7:5)? Well, now Rahab knew as well.

Rahab Makes a Covenant

After she made known her decision to follow the God of Israel, she made a covenant with the men on her rooftop. She offered to help them to safety if they would spare her and her family when they came in to overthrow Jericho. These are the words of her plea:

Please swear to me by the Lord, since I have dealt kindly with you, that you also will deal kindly with my father's household, and give me a pledge of truth, and spare my father and my mother and my brothers and my sisters, with all who belong to them, and deliver our lives from death.

The spies agreed to this covenant and offered the pledge of their very lives to deal kindly and faithfully with her and her family if she promised to conceal what they were doing and helped them to escape.

Rahab proceeded to let them down by a rope through her window on the wall. She gave them instructions on where to hide in the hill country for three days until their pursuers returned. The further instructions to her by the Israelite men forever stand as a highlighted symbol and spiritual sign for all mankind. They told her to tie a scarlet cord in her window so that the invading army would recognize her house, deliver the inhabitants, and spare them from destruction.

The Israelite men said to Rahab,

We shall be free from this oath to you which you have made us swear, unless, when we come into the land, you tie this cord of scarlet thread in the window through which you let us down, and gather to yourself into the house your father and your mother and your brothers and all your father's household. It shall come about that anyone who goes out of the doors of your house into the street, his blood shall be on his own head, and we shall be free; but anyone who is with you in the house, his blood shall be on our head if a hand is laid on him. (Joshua 2:17ff)

Doesn't this remind you of the Passover? In actuality, it has been referred to as the "second Passover." The scarlet cord immediately evokes the imagery of the blood of Christ. At the time of the Exodus from Egypt, the Lord had instructed the head of each Hebrew household in Egypt to slay a lamb and apply the blood over the lintel and doorposts of their houses. In this way the Lord would pass over the door and would not allow the "Destroyer" to come into the house to slay their firstborn. None of the members of the household were allowed to go outside the door until morning. Under the protection of the blood, whole families were saved, and in the case of Rahab, her whole family was saved when Joshua and the two men who had spied out the land saw the scarlet cord.

This further revelation of the Family covenant through Rahab is a treasure given to us by the Lord. It is a profound picture of the covenant that God makes with each of us, and that covenant includes our families. God gave the promise to Abraham and to his children after him that He would be their God (Genesis 17:7). This promise is also given in the New Testament. "For the promise is unto you and to your children, and to all who are afar off, even as many as the Lord our God shall call" (Acts 2:39). The story of Rahab gives us a clear understanding of God's heart of lovingkindness. He wants to save whole families. Rahab teaches us that we should boldly claim the salvation of our family before the throne of God. Unfortunately the seed of the serpent vies for our children. It is of paramount importance that we take the responsibility to train and teach our children the ways of the Lord and testify of His wondrous works in our lives. Rahab models for us that the family covenant works the other way around too. She spearheads the way for passionate intercession for the eternal salvation of our extended families. If you urgently tried to persuade your grown children, your unbelieving spouse, your mother and father, your brothers and sisters to join you under the shelter of the scarlet cord and under the shelter of the blood to save them from certain eternal death, would they come? Maybe we have some work to do to clear the way (through forgiveness, reconciliation, and acts of love) for them to enter the family covenant of God.

We are constrained to intercede continually for our families. Because of the lure of this sinful world, free will, and the serpent, the battle for our loved ones to enter in is always before us. Yet we know the Father's heart. We know He has yearned for sons and daughters to join His Holy Covenant before the beginning of time. As we fight for our families, He is on our side.

The Scarlet Cord

As Rahab tied the scarlet cord outside her window three thousand years ago, God knew that this act would be significant for all time. Rahab stands as a torchbearer for all of us who believe in the "Lord our God, who is God in heaven above and on the earth beneath," as she did. She was a forerunner of faith and gave those of us who are Gentiles a foretaste of the redemption that would be ours through Christ. The scarlet cord was the pledge that the spies would fulfill the covenant they had made with her. At that point she could do nothing more than trust in it. Yet the scarlet cord depicted more than the saving of Rahab and her family. It is threaded through the Old Covenant and into the New until it reaches and mingles with the scarlet cord of blood running from the pierced side of the crucified Christ. As Gentile Christians rejoice in the scarlet cord at the cross, it is imperative that they also remember the scarlet cord on Rahab's window with gratitude. Rahab regarded the Jews to be God's firstborn son, which God had hoped all the pagan nations would do, risking everything to worship their Covenant God. Rahab was an instrument in God's hands to save the lives of the Hebrew spies, prepare the way for the Israelites to conquer Jericho, and expedite their long-awaited entry into the Promised Land. Because of her faith and obedience, God has honored her throughout these many centuries. The story of Rahab concludes with the statement that Joshua spared Rahab and her father's household and all she had, "and she has lived in the midst of Israel to this day." Yet her story does not really conclude in the Book of Joshua. She is listed in Hebrews 11 in the "Hall of Faith." "By faith Rahab the harlot did not perish along with those who were disobedient, after she had welcomed the spies in peace" (Hebrews 11:31).

She is also mentioned in James 2:25. "In the same way, was not Rahab the harlot also justified by works when she received the messengers and sent them out by another way?"

For those who are unfamiliar with the Bible, it could be startling to read the genealogy of Jesus the Messiah in the first chapter of Matthew. These names are included in the long list of ancestors of Jesus: Salmon was the father of Boaz by Rahab, Boaz was the father of Obed by Ruth, and Obed was the father of Jesse. Jesse was the father of David the king. Check it out for yourself! Isn't it amazing? Talk about honor!

The Lord Exalts Joshua in the Sight of the People

When the spies returned, they told Joshua about the vow they had made with Rahab, assuring him that the Lord had given them the land and that all the inhabitants of the land had been demoralized before them. Joshua set out with the sons of Israel and came to the edge of the Jordan River. He spoke to the priests and told them to take up the ark of the covenant and cross over ahead of the people. The Lord spoke to Joshua privately and said, "This day I will begin to exalt you in the sight of all Israel, that they may know that just as I have been with Moses, I will be with you." Joshua declared to the people that by what was going to happen, they would know that the living God was among them. When the feet of the priests who carried the ark of the covenant rested in the waters of the Jordan, the waters of the Jordan were cut off, and the waters that were flowing down from above stood in one heap. The priests who carried the ark of the covenant of the Lord stood firm on dry ground in the middle of the Jordan, while all of Israel crossed on dry ground until they reached the other side opposite Jericho. When the Lord had delivered them out of bondage from Egypt, He had miraculously parted the Red Sea, and now as He brought His chosen people into the land He had promised them, He miraculously parted the Jordan River. The Lord commanded Joshua to choose twelve men to take up twelve stones out of the middle of the Jordan from the place where the priests feet were standing firm and put them down in their lodging place for the night. Then Joshua commanded the men to cross again to the ark and set up twelve stones in the middle of the Jordan, where the feet of the priests who carried the ark of the covenant were standing. Joshua said,

> Let this be a sign among you, so that when your children ask later, saying, "What do these stones mean to you?" Then you shall say to them, "Because the waters of the Jordan were cut off before the ark of the covenant of the Lord; when it crossed the Jordan, the waters were cut off." So these stones shall become a memorial to the sons of Israel forever.

In Josh. 4:9, this statement is made: "And they are there to this day." (Maybe an ambitious archaeologist will find them someday.)

Perhaps we should be more mindful of collecting reminders of the mighty acts of deliverance, healing, and answered prayer that the Lord has done in our lives. Our nation erects statues and libraries to memorialize great men. Many write memoirs and publish biographies. We collect pictures and create scrapbooks of our children. We are diligent in designing headstones at the graves of our loved ones. It appears that we are less faithful in commemorating the miraculous interventions of the Lord in our lives. Even some of our grand and elaborate churches seem to be built more to the glory of man than to God. In His infinite wisdom, God understands that finite man needs some tangible, visible signs to remind them of His infinite power and lovingkindness. He gave us the rainbow in the sky, the waters of baptism, and the cross of Calvary. To his disciples he gave wine in a cup and said, "This cup which is poured out for you is the new covenant in my blood." He also gave them bread and said, "This is my body which is given for you; do this in remembrance of Me." It can't be clearer than that. Certainly we should be ready with an answer when our sons ask us, "What do these *stones* (whatever they may be) mean to you?"

The Scriptures record that through these wonders, the Lord exalted Joshua in the sight of all the people so that they revered him just as they had revered Moses. Moses would be a hard act to follow in the leadership of about three million people; however, Joshua was chosen by God, and God elevated him and prepared the way for him to undertake his appointed role.

When Joshua was by Jericho, he lifted his eyes to behold a man standing opposite him, with his sword drawn in his hand. Joshua went to him and asked, "Are you for us or for our adversaries?" The man answered that he had come as the captain of the host of the Lord. This was an astounding answer, and Joshua immediately recognized that this divine commander was here not only to fight for him but to lead a host of heavenly warriors on Israel's behalf. What a relief it must have been! What a weight lifted off his shoulders! One of God's promises in His covenant with the Israelites was this:

> Behold, I am going to send an angel before you to guard you along the way and to bring you into the place which I have prepared. If you truly obey his voice and do all that I say, then I will be an enemy to your enemies and an adversary to your adversaries. (Exodus 23:22)

This promise in the Holy Scriptures is for us today too. God's covenantal relationship with His people is for all time, and He Himself never changes. As we face the Jericho walls of life, we have access to our Heavenly Father through Jesus, and He sends His legions of ministering angels to help us. We are not alone.

Joshua immediately fell on his face in an attitude of humility and reverence and asked if this captain of the Lord's host had anything to say to him. The answer was that he should remove his sandals from his feet, for he was standing on holy ground. Joshua did so just like Moses did at the burning bush.

Before he took his people on to the conquest of Canaan, Joshua shepherded them through some acts of preparation. The Lord had told him to circumcise the sons of Israel a second time. This was important because circumcision was a response to the covenant God had made with Abraham and a sign of the covenant. It also was declarative that the covenant was not only for them but for their seed. The males who had been circumcised when they came out of Egypt wandered in the wilderness for forty years and all died in the wilderness. The parents of the children born in the wilderness had not had their children circumcised, so Joshua saw to it that this act was done before they entered the Promised Land. Again we see the disobedience and negligence of the prior generation. On the desert plains of Jericho Joshua also led his people in the celebration of the Passover on the evening of the fourteenth day of the month. This Passover rite was another gift from God to remind them in a tangible way of God's deliverance from the bondage of Egypt. God had said to them in Egypt,

> You shall observe this event as an ordinance for you and your children forever. When you enter the land which the Lord will give you, as He has promised, you shall observe this rite. And when your children say to you, "What does this rite mean to you?" you shall say, "It is a Passover sacrifice to the Lord who passed over the houses of the sons of Israel

in Egypt when He smote the Egyptians, but spared your homes." (Exodus 12:24)

On the day after the Passover the sons of Israel ate some of the produce of the land and unleavened cakes and grain. The miraculous provision of manna ceased, and they ate of the yield of the land of Canaan thereafter.

The Walls Came Tumbling Down

The battle of Jericho is well-known throughout biblical history because of its dramatic context and the improbability of destroying such a fortification. The archeologists have confirmed that the double walls were virtually impregnable. On the basis of evidence, they have supported the biblical account that the walls did indeed come tumbling down. In fact, many details of the siege have been authenticated by the uncovering of the rubble of the ancient city. God had been explicit in telling the Israelites that they could take no plunder for themselves, as was the custom, for the land was the Lord's. They could take only the silver and gold and articles of bronze and iron, which should be put in the treasury of the house of the Lord. This siege would have taken place right after the harvest, and many large jars of grain were found among the ruins, many that were highly valued and were used in bartering and trade at the time. This indicated also that though the inhabitants of Jericho could have held out for at least a year or two, the invasion must have been of very short duration (such as a seven day period).

God gave a definite battle plan to Joshua. This plan was certainly one of a kind (Joshua 6:5). Seven priests with seven trumpets of rams' horns were to lead a procession around Jericho, carrying the ark of the covenant. The six hundred thousand armed men of the Israelites, the twelve tribes, were to follow silently behind. They were to repeat this march once each day for six days. On the seventh day they were commanded to circle the city seven times, and this day the priests were to blow their trumpets. At the end of this procession when the priests blew a long blast on their trumpets, the people were told to shout with a great shout, and the walls of the city of Jericho would fall down. Much conjecture has been offered by skeptics and scientists as to just how those walls fell down. This verse in Hebrews 11:30 answers that question so simply: "By faith the walls of Jericho fell down after they had been encircled for seven days." Without a doubt, the captain of the host of the Lord, with the sword drawn in his hand, who had appeared to Joshua before the battle of Jericho, had marched in with his hosts to demolish the walls. Would this have happened if Joshua and the Israelites had not believed the Word of the Lord and disobeyed His instructions? What would have been the outcome if they had tried their own strategies in the effort to infiltrate Jericho? Knowing what we know about the covenants with God, we see that heaven and earth work together to achieve God's purposes. God needed believing men on earth like Noah, Abraham, Moses, and Joshua to carry out His redemptive plans. God chose to do it this way, working in concert with man.

In a German excavation from 1907 to 1909, it was discovered that a portion of the north wall did not fall as it did everywhere else. It was still standing to a height of about eight feet, and amazingly there were still houses built against that wall! The city wall formed the back wall of the houses, and it is certainly possible that this is where Rahab's house was located. We know that when the Israelites climbed up over the fallen walls of Jericho, Joshua told the two spies to "go into the harlot's house and bring the woman and all she has out of there, as you have sworn to her. So they went in and brought out Rahab and her father and her mother and her brothers and all she had; they also brought out all her relatives and placed them outside the camp of Israel" (Joshua 6:22).

The Lord Gives Israel the Land

As the mighty warrior who was chosen by God, Joshua led his armies into the land of Canaan and conquered the southern and northern regions of Canaan, battle by battle. It is recorded in the Scriptures that there was not a city that made peace with the sons of Israel (except the Hivites living in Gibeon). They overtook them all in battle. In Joshua 21:43, this historic period is summed up this way:

> So the Lord gave Israel all the land which He had sworn to give to their fathers, and they possessed it and lived in it. And the Lord gave them rest on every side, according to all that He had sworn to their fathers, and no one of all their enemies stood before them; the Lord gave all their enemies into their hand. Not one of the good promises which the Lord had made to the house of Israel failed, all came to pass.

The Twelve Tribes of Israel

As we turn the pages of covenantal history, we should keep in mind that from the beginning God has used families to be intrinsically involved in His plans and purposes. When we read the words "the twelve tribes of Israel," we should be aware that this phrase could just as easily be recorded as "the twelve families of Israel." The nation of Israel was formed from the twelve sons of Jacob, and to this day it is made up of the descendants of these twelve brothers. The Jews as a nation emerged from Jacob's (Israel's) children and often are referred to as the "children of Israel." Remember that the promises of the covenant always include the future descendants and generations. Who were familiar descendants of these twelve brothers? We immediately recognize Samson, who descended from Gad. Saul, the first king of Israel, and Esther, the queen of Persia, both of whom were descendants of Benjamin, also come to mind. Moses and Aaron were from the family of Levi, and John the Baptist also descended from Levi. King

David was a descendant of Judah, and we know that Jesus was also born of that lineage. The importance of these historical figures in the Bible, who were so instrumental in moving along God's plan of salvation and reconciliation, didn't end when they ended! In the past we may have relegated them to history and immortalized them in the Old Testament. God retains them in the continuing saga of His redemption and has another perspective on their place in His heart and in His ongoing story. In Luke 22:30, Jesus says to His disciples,

> You are those who have stood by Me in My trials; and just as My Father has granted Me a kingdom, I grant you that you may eat and drink at My table in My kingdom, and you will sit on thrones judging the twelve tribes of Israel.

In the Book of Revelation, John saw the "holy city, Jerusalem, coming down out of heaven from God, having the glory of God. Her brilliance was like a very costly stone, as a stone of crystal-clear jasper. It had a great and high wall, with twelve gates, and at the gates twelve angels; and names were written on them, which are the names of the twelve tribes of the sons of Israel" (Revelation 21:12).

These words show the everlasting, unfailing love of the Father for His people, for His families, for His tribes. When we speak of the covenant God makes with families, we are speaking of something eternal that never passes away.

Joshua performed amazing military feats in Canaan, leading his armies into victory after victory until the children of Israel could claim the land and settle there. This conquest took seven years. Canaan was for Israel to conquer, but it belonged to the Lord. It was understood from the beginning that the land would be cleansed from all remnants of paganism and idolatry and that the people of God would remain faithful to the one true God and be a witness and a testimony to the nations. Joshua was God's chosen servant to complete the mission of Moses, establish the children of Israel in the Promised Land, and divide the land among the tribes. "So Joshua took the whole land, according to all that the Lord had spoken to Moses, and Joshua gave it for an inheritance to Israel according to their divisions by their tribes" (Joshua 11:23).

The Faithfulness of God

Some of the Canaanite nations still remained in the land, but the Lord had promised that He would drive them out from before them. When Joshua was old and advanced in years, he delivered a farewell address to the people, urging them to be firm, and to do all that was written in the law of Moses. He warned them not to associate with the nations that remained and especially not to serve or bow down to their gods or intermarry. The Lord their God would not continue to drive these nations out from before them if they allowed them to become a snare to them. Then Joshua delivered these amazing words, which should resonate in our hearts too as we look back on what the Lord has done for us:

> You know in all your hearts and in all your souls that not one word of all the good words which the Lord your God spoke concerning you has failed; all have been fulfilled for you, not one of them has failed. (Joshua 23:14)

What a good and faithful God we have! His faithfulness is overwhelming when we look back about seven hundred years to the time when God promised Abraham that He would give to him a land and make of Him a great nation and that in him all the families of the earth would be blessed! It should assure us that even when we can't understand the big picture of what is happening in our world today, our God has a plan that He is fulfilling. Every word He has spoken to us through the Bible, through prophecy, and through the Holy Spirit into our hearts will come to pass. Not one word or promise will fail.

After Joshua reminded the children of Israel about the faithfulness of God, he gathered all the tribes of Israel to Shechem and called for the elders of Israel and for their heads, judges, and officers. He admonished them again not to transgress the covenant of the Lord because if they served other gods and bowed down to them, then the anger of the Lord would burn against them. Toward the end of his address he reviewed the history of Israel and highlighted the many sovereign acts of God on their behalf. As Joshua continued, it became apparent that he struggled with the fear that Israel would stray from the Lord after he was gone. He guided them into the making of another covenant. Just as the people had readily agreed to obey God when Moses presented the terms of the Mosaic Covenant, they responded to the terms of this covenant by saying, "Far be it from us that we should forsake the Lord to serve other gods" (Joshua 24:16). Joshua still had his misgivings. He said, "You are witnesses against yourselves that you have chosen for yourselves the Lord, to serve Him" (Joshua 24:22). The people shouted, "We are witnesses! We will serve the Lord our God and we will obey His voice." Joshua wrote these words in the book of the law of God (Joshua 24:26).

The curtain falls as Joshua takes a large stone and sets it up under the oak that was by the sanctuary of the Lord. He says to the people, "Behold, this stone shall be for a witness against us, for it has heard all the words of the Lord which He spoke to us; thus it shall be for a witness against you, so that you do not deny your God."

Then Joshua dismisses the people, each to his own inheritance.

In the high priestly prayer of Jesus in John 17:4, He says to the Father, "I glorified You on the earth, having accomplished the work which You have given Me to do."

Surely this is also true of Joshua.

CHAPTER 14

FROM THE PASTURE TO THE THRONE

The curtain rises on a man named Samuel, a great judge and prophet of Israel, as he journeys to the town of Bethlehem to meet with the family of Jesse. He has been instructed to fill his horn with oil and go to the house of Jesse in order to anoint a king of the Lord's choosing from among Jesse's sons. Much had happened since the death of Joshua, and the misgivings Joshua had expressed about Israel's obedience to the covenant of God and serving the gods of the Canaanites had been realized. The Scriptures inform us in Judges 2:10 that the following generation that arose after Joshua died did not know the Lord or the work He had done on their behalf. In Judges 2:11, these words are recorded:

> Then the sons of Israel did evil in the sight of the Lord and served the Baals, and they forsook the Lord, the God of their fathers, who had brought them out of Egypt, and followed other Gods from among the gods of the peoples who were around them, and bowed down to them, and thus provoked the Lord to anger.

The anointed leadership of Joshua was replaced by a series of twelve judges who were ineffectual in guiding and preserving the people as a "light to the nations." The Israelites did not fare well with a decentralized leadership. The nation fell into sin, suffered the consequences, and cried out to the Lord for mercy, and then the pattern would begin all over again. The judges ruled according to their own evil wills, and the people floundered in the sea of their own independence and waywardness. The Book of Judges ends with this sad statement: "In those days there was no king in Israel; everyone did what was right in his own eyes" (Judges 21:25).

Of course, from the beginning the understanding had been that the Lord would be their king, but this understanding had long been forgotten. The people began asking Samuel for a king, pleading to be like other nations that had kings to judge them, ones who went out before them to fight their battles. The people of Israel had no desire to be a shining model for other nations by submitting to the rule of the Most High God, and trusting Him to conquer their enemies.

When Samuel unburdened his troubled heart to the Lord, He was told, "Listen to the voice of the people in regard to all that they say to you, for they have not rejected you, but they have rejected Me from being king over them" (1 Samuel 8:7).

After God told Samuel to inform the people of the dangers and obligations that were contingent in the appointment of a king, apprising them of the cost in time and money, and heard their reply, "No, but there shall be a king over us" (1 Samuel 8:19), He told him to grant the wishes of the people and to anoint Saul as king over Israel.

God Grants Israel a King

Later the people pleaded with Samuel to pray for them so that they would not die, for they had "added to all their sins this evil, by asking for themselves a king" (1 Samuel 12:19). Samuel assured them that the Lord would not abandon them "on account of His great name, because the Lord has been pleased to make you a people for Himself" (1 Samuel 12:19–22). It is always baffling to see God's unceasing love and faithfulness in the face of such sin and apostasy! Samuel also promised that he would never sin against the Lord by ceasing to pray for them or failing to instruct them in the ways of truth.

In the end God granted the people a king who was of His own choosing, who was anointed by Samuel, and who was imparted with the Spirit. In other words, the king of Israel was an under-king with the sovereign, divine King ruling over him. The prophetic counsel of Samuel provided checks and balances to the kingship. God's intention was that the new king would set the bar for the Israelites to live up to the expectations of the covenant and to be a light to the nations. This was the God-given mandate of the king.

Despite all this preparatory initiation and inauguration of the king of Israel, Samuel was now on his way to anoint another king because the first king didn't work out so well. At first Saul was successful in his acceptance by the people and his military pursuits, but eventually his disobedience to the Lord caused his kingship to fail. When told to utterly destroy the Amalekites and all that they had, he spared Agag, the king of the Amalekites, and confiscated the best of the sheep, the oxen, the fatlings, the lambs, and all that was good. Samuel said to Saul, "Because you have rejected the word of the Lord, He has rejected you as king" (1 Samuel 15:23). This did not mean that Saul was immediately dethroned. Rather, it meant that whereas the Lord would have established his kingdom forever, now his kingdom would not endure. Samuel explained that "the Lord has sought out for Himself a man after His own heart, and has appointed him as ruler over His people, because you have not kept what the Lord commanded you" (1 Samuel 13:14).

Samuel Anoints Another King

The Lord told Samuel to fill his horn with oil and go to Jesse the Bethlehemite in order to anoint a king from Jesse's sons, one whom the Lord would designate to him. As Jesse brought seven of his sons to pass one by one before Samuel, the Lord indicated that none of them were His choice for a king. Samuel asked if Jesse had any other sons, and the answer was that the youngest was tending the sheep in the pasture. When David was brought in, the Lord said to Samuel, "Arise, anoint him, for this is he." Samuel took the horn of oil and anointed him, and the Spirit of the Lord came mightily upon David from that day forward. David was about sixteen years old at the time.

As we look back on the ancient history of Israel, certain aspects of God's plan to restore creation to Himself become recognizable to us. We are aware that He repeatedly chose specific servants to carry out His plan, and it is fascinating when we know that He had chosen them to be part of His plan from before the beginning of time. Some were chosen as infants, such as Moses and Jesus, and one was chosen as a shepherd lad (such as David) to carry out assignments that would affect eternity! We are constantly reminded in the pages of Scripture that the Lord's focus is on families, lineages, and generations in the drama of His ongoing salvation/restoration plan. Our covenant God continually contended with rebellion, disobedience, and the perverse, contrary ways of mankind, and yet His will prevailed because of His everlasting covenant. The following prophecies were written four hundred to a thousand years before they were fulfilled, appearing along the way as prophetic road signs assuring the traveler that he was going in the right direction.

> But as for you, Bethlehem (formerly, Ephrathah) too little to be among the clans of Judah, from you One will go forth for Me to be ruler in Israel. His goings forth are from long ago from the days of eternity. (Micah 5:2)

Consider the following as well: "Then a shoot will spring from the stem of Jesse and a branch from his roots will bear fruit. The Spirit of the Lord will rest on Him" (Isaiah 11:1).

A further prophecy in Jeremiah 23:5–6 reads, "Behold, the days are coming," declares the Lord, when I will raise up for David a righteous Branch, and He will reign as king and act wisely and do justice and righteousness in the land."

What a comfort it is to know that God is sovereign and has everything under His control despite the age-old efforts of the serpent and men everywhere to override His plans.

> He spoke, and it was done; He commanded, and it stood fast. The Lord nullifies the counsel of the nations; He frustrates the plans of the peoples. The counsel of the Lord stands forever, the plans of His heart from generation to generation. (Psalms 33:9–11)

David and Goliath

As a young boy, David already showed signs of being a "man after God's own heart" (Acts 13:22). Whereas nations and kings could not comprehend the covenant of God and could not bring themselves to trust the God of the covenant, David declared his understanding of the covenant with his words and his actions at such a young age! The Philistines had gathered their armies in battle, and Saul and his men of Israel were camped opposite them in the valley. A champion of the Philistines, a giant named Goliath, stepped out from the ranks and shouted, "Why do you come out to draw up in battle array? Am I not the Philistine, and you the servants of Saul? Choose a man for yourselves and let him come down to me" (1 Samuel 17:8). The men of Israel fled from the man in fear. David asked this question of the men, "For who is this uncircumcised Philistine, that he should taunt the armies of the living God?" (1 Samuel 17:26). David accepted the challenge to fight against this champion of the Philistines, this giant Goliath, single-handedly. Despite King Saul's protests that he was too young, David's reply was, "The Lord who delivered me from the paw of the lion and from the paw of the bear, will deliver me from the hand of this Philistine" (1 Samuel 17:37). David took his stick in his hand and five smooth stones from the brook and put them in his shepherd's bag, and his sling was in his hand as he approached Goliath. The giant scorned and ridiculed David and cursed him by his gods. With divine revelation of the covenant that God had made with Israel, David cried out,

> You come to me with a sword, a spear, and a javelin, but I come to you in the name of the Lord of hosts, the God of the armies of Israel, whom you have taunted. This day the Lord will deliver you up into my hands ... that all the earth may know that there is a god in Israel and that all this assembly may know that the Lord does not deliver by sword or by spear; for the battle is the Lord's and He will give you into our hands. (Samuel 17:45ff)

This is the covenant of God in a nutshell! David understood. In Exodus 23:22, God had promised the Israelites that He would be an enemy to their enemies and an adversary to their adversaries. God is a covenant God and is always faithful to what He promises. David simply believed the Lord and took Him at His word just like Abraham had done so many years before. David also recalled the times in his young life while he was out tending his father's sheep when God had delivered him from the attacks of wild animals. He concluded that if God had rescued him then, He surely would prevail for him over this Philistine now.

Knowing what we know about the faithful character of God our Father and the unchangeable course of His plan for the salvation of the world and remembering what He has done in our personal lives to provide all that we need and to defend us all along the way, how can we doubt His power when we are faced with seemingly insurmountable challenges? Sometimes we don't draw everything together to stand on the firm foundation of faith. We face our enemies alone in unbelief and trepidation. In Ephesians 2, Paul refers to the Gentiles as once being "separate from Christ, excluded from the commonwealth of Israel, and strangers to the covenants of promise, having no hope and without God in the world." The key is our understanding and faith in the covenant that God has made with us. On His own initiative and out of His love for us, God entered into covenant with man, and since He could swear by no one greater, He swore by Himself. What more can He do? It is impossible for God to lie.

David triumphed over the Philistine with a sling and a stone. He killed him, and there was no sword in David's hand. It is reminiscent of Psalm 33:16.

> The king is not saved by a mighty army;
> A warrior is not delivered by great strength.
> A horse is a false hope for victory;
> Nor does it deliver anyone by its great strength.
> Behold, the eye of the Lord is on those who fear Him,
> On those who hope for His lovingkindness.

In Acts 13:22, Paul addresses the men of Israel and says, "God raised up David to be their king, concerning whom He also testified and said, 'I have found David, the son of Jesse, a man after my own heart, who will do all my will.' From the descendants of this man, according to the promise, God has brought to Israel a Savior, Jesus." David is referred to as "a man after God's own heart" not because he was always righteous but because he understood the covenant. He had carried in his shepherd's bag a stone, a sling, and a simple, unswerving faith in the God of the covenant.

The Covenant of David and Jonathan

King Saul asked David to live in the palace after he slayed Goliath, and in the course of time David and Jonathan, Saul's son, became intimate friends. The Bible describes the relationship this way: "The soul of Jonathan was knit to the soul of David, and Jonathan loved him as himself" (1 Samuel 18:1). The covenant between them that ensued was a common ritual in the eastern countries of that day, and it has been described in an earlier section of this book. Two people entering into covenant exchanged vows and other personal belongings and thereby made a promise that everything they possessed (including their children) was given to the other. Jonathan, the son of the king, gave his robe to David (signifying his personhood) as well as his armor, his sword, his bow, and his belt (which represented his strength). When David suspected that King Saul planned to kill him because of jealousy over his celebrity after he had killed Goliath and David's obvious favor with God, Jonathan agreed to investigate the matter and set a time to meet David in a field to disclose what he had discovered. When the truth was evident that David must flee for his life, both of these friends kissed each other and wept together. Jonathan said to David, "Go in safety inasmuch as we have sworn to each other in the name of the Lord, saying, "The Lord will be between me and you, and between my descendants and your descendants forever" (1 Samuel 20:42).

King Saul Pursues David

After the prophet Samuel had anointed David as the king of Israel, about fourteen years passed before he actually was crowned king at the age of thirty. David spent much of this time running and hiding in the wilderness as a fugitive in an effort to escape the relentless pursuit of King Saul. Even though King Saul had been rejected by God because of his disobedience, he had not yet been removed from the throne. David also assembled an army of mighty men, approximately four hundred in number, and clashed with the army of Saul several times; however, David would not touch "the Lord's anointed" and repeatedly showed kindness to the king. It became clear that David knew that his God would bring justice to bear on Saul, and though he was under the continual threat of death himself, he did not seek to end Saul's life. At one time David saw the place where Saul had encamped as he malevolently followed David. In the night David and one of his men, Abishai, went down to the center of the camp where Saul was sleeping, surrounded by all his army. Looking down at the sleeping Saul, with his spear stuck in the ground at his head and his jug of water nearby, Abishai was eager to end King Saul's life in a single stroke, but David said,

> Do not destroy him, for who can stretch out his hand against the Lord's anointed and be without guilt? As the Lord lives, surely the Lord will strike him, or his day will come that he dies, or he will go down into battle and perish. But now please take the spear that is at his head, and the jug of water, and let us go. (1 Samuel 26:9)

Although David is our model for a man of faith who drew great strength from the covenant and applied its meaning to his everyday life, he also cried out to the Lord in His distress and asked the Lord to hasten His help. When he was hiding in a cave, he wrote Psalm 142, pouring out his complaint before the Lord, declaring his trouble before Him, asking Him to deliver him from his persecutors and to bring his soul out of prison. He had no doubt that God would answer all his prayers. Here is another sample from Psalms 57:1–3:

> Be gracious to me, O God, be gracious to me,
> for my soul takes refuge in You;
> and in the shadow of Your wings I will take refuge until destruction passes by.

> I will cry to God Most High,
> to God who accomplishes all things for me.
> He will send from heaven and save me.
> He reproaches him who tramples upon me.
>
> God will send forth His lovingkindness and
> His truth.

The word *lovingkindness* is a covenant word. It is used in the Bible 176 times and refers to God's lovingkindness expressed in His covenant relationship with Israel. It expresses God's loyalty to His covenant and His love for His people along with a faithfulness to keep His promises. The depth of the word extends into the future and is latent with blessings for generations to come. Here is an example in Psalm 103:17:

> But the lovingkindness of the Lord
> is from everlasting to everlasting
> on those who fear Him,
> and His righteousness to children's children,
> to those who keep His covenant
> and remember His precepts to do them.

It is interesting to me that when I write the word *lovingkindness* on my computer, it is automatically underlined in red. The computer doesn't recognize the word. It is from the vocabulary of the living God.

In a battle with the Philistines, the men of Israel fled from before them and fell slain on Mount Gilboa. The account in the Bible says that the Philistines overtook Saul and three of his sons, including Jonathan, and killed them. Saul actually was hit by the archers and was badly wounded. In the end he fell on his sword and took his own life.

The Men of Judah Anoint David King

The men of Judah anointed David king, and he ruled over the house of Judah in Hebron for seven years and six months. After a long civil war between the House of Saul and the House of David and indecision among some of the tribes as to who should replace Saul, all the tribes of Israel finally came to David at Hebron and said, "We are your bone and your flesh" (2 Samuel 5:1). In other words, they were family, and they would follow him. They declared that the Lord had appointed him to shepherd His people and that the time was at hand for him to rule over Israel. King David made a covenant with them, and they anointed him as king over the twelve tribes of Israel. David was thirty years old at the time, and he reigned for forty years. God helped David wherever he went, and he ruled over all his people in righteousness and justice.

The Story of Mephibosheth

After the death of Saul and his sons, the Lord gave the Israelites a level of peace that they hadn't experienced for a long time. When David took the throne, he remembered the covenant he had made with Jonathan, Saul's son. He had not forgotten the love he had for Jonathan or the fact that this covenant was binding from generation to generation. In fact, the vow they had sworn to one another was, "The Lord will be between me and you, and between my descendants and your descendants" (1 Samuel 20:42). So David asked if anyone was left of the House of Saul so that he could show kindness for Jonathan's sake. One of the inherent vows of the covenant is that "everything I have is yours and everything you have is mine." An old servant of the household named Ziba told him that there was still a son of Jonathan named Mephibosheth, who was crippled in both feet. Years before when it was apparent that David would take the throne and the House of Saul was coming down, a nurse had picked up the five-year-old Mephibosheth and fled. She had believed all of Saul's lies about David being the cause of the problems in the land, and she was convinced that David would kill them all. In her haste she fell and dropped the child, and he had been lame ever since. He had lived all these years as an outcast in a far-off place called Lo-debar.

When Mephibosheth was brought before David, he fell prostrate before him. The son of Jonathan expected either to be executed or taken as a prisoner of war. This was a customary practice so that the survivors of the prior king's family could pose no future threat to the new king. David, however, said,

> Do not fear, for I will surely show kindness to you for the sake of your father, Jonathan, and will restore to you all the land of your grandfather Saul; and you shall eat at my table regularly. (2 Samuel 9:7)

The response of Mephibosheth was, "What is your servant, that you should regard a dead dog like me?" (2 Samuel 9:8).

The Bible concludes this story by saying, "So Mephibosheth ate at David's table as one of the king's sons" (2 Samuel 9:11). What a descriptive portrayal this is of what a covenant is when it is made between two people! Not only did lovingkindness bind them together for the rest of their lives, but it extended to the next generation.

Jerusalem as the "City of David"

When David was anointed king over all of Israel, he again gave *us* an insight into *His* insight in regard to the covenant of God with Israel. David knew from the time God had taken him from shepherding the sheep and had brought him to shepherding His chosen people that this was a momentous time in the redemptive restoration of all that God had promised to Abraham. He seemed aware that his life as he lived it and his reign as he reigned on the throne would constitute a significant stepping stone to that promise (Psalms 78:70–71). David proceeded to take his men to Jerusalem, and he captured the stronghold of Zion, which has since been known as the "City of David." Up until that time David's capital had been among the southern tribes in Hebron, but Jerusalem was more centrally located between the southern and northern tribes and more conducive to establishing the unity of Israel. Also at this time David gathered thirty thousand of his chosen men and brought the ark of God from Baale-judah to Jerusalem and placed it in a tent that David had pitched for it. In this way he testified to the nation that it was God who was their ruler. It was the God of the covenant who was their king, and David would rule under His auspices as His representative.

In the midst of the miraculous chain of events in David's life, he could well have been filled with personal pride and euphoria. Just as God had made Abraham's name great, so He had made David's name great. In 1 Samuel 5:10, the Scriptures tell us that "David became greater and greater, for the Lord God of hosts was with him." Yet this was David's perspective on all of this: "And David realized that the Lord had established him as king over Israel, and that He had exalted his kingdom for the sake of His people Israel" (2 Samuel 5:11).

No wonder God called David a man after His own heart! David understood that all the events leading up to the establishment of his throne were aligned with the plan of God from all eternity to restore humanity to Himself. David knew in his heart that he was simply a man chosen by God to fulfill his part of the plan, which God was unfolding before his very eyes. It must have been an overwhelming revelation for David to realize that God's promise to Abraham, Isaac, and Jacob and the spoken secrets of His heart to Moses when He had talked with him face-to-face were now in the process of being fulfilled. The promise of a seed to Abraham was now more readily anticipated through David's lineage.

God Chooses Solomon to Build His Temple

When David was situated in his house in Jerusalem, he told Nathan the prophet that he desired to build a house for the Lord. He didn't think it was appropriate for him to live in a house of cedar, while the ark of the covenant resided in tent curtains. David had in mind a glorious temple that reflected the beauty and majesty of God. He wanted a habitation for the Lord that far surpassed in splendor any edifice built for men. God responded to this request by informing David that he would not be the one who would build Him a house because he was a man of war and had shed much blood on the earth. Rather, God would choose his son, Solomon, a man of peace, to build His temple.

David was given the pleasure and honor of submitting all the plans, preparations, and materials for the building of the temple to his son, Solomon. Included in his plans were its storehouses, its courtyards, its upper rooms and inner rooms, and the room for the mercy seat. He set stonecutters to prepare dressed stones and brought in stores of iron for nails, loads of bronze that could not be weighed, and cedar timbers without number. Solomon began to build the temple in the 480th year after the people of Israel came out of the land of Egypt.

With the completion of the temple, the ritual of sacrifices of animals for the atonement of sins became of central importance in the lives of the Israelites. On the fourteenth day of the first month, people from all over Israel would come to Jerusalem to celebrate the Passover by bringing or purchasing their lambs for sacrifice. They joined the throngs lined up in the temple toward the altar. At the designated time they slit the throats of their lambs, and the Levite facing each one of them caught the blood in a basin and passed it along the line of Levites toward the altar to eventually be sprinkled against the altar. A trail of blood for the atonement of sin continued to flow through the grandeur of the temple and the new sanctuary. It was also a time of joyous worship and praise to God, as the people sang and danced to trumpets, cymbals, flutes, and other musical instruments. These festivities continued as each family roasted their lambs in the ovens prepared throughout Jerusalem for this purpose. In the evening all of Israel ate the Passover meal in an atmosphere of unity.

A portion of Solomon's dedication of the temple as he spread out his hands toward heaven is as follows:

> O Lord, the God of Israel, there is no God like You in heaven above or on earth beneath, keeping covenant and showing lovingkindness to Your servants who walk before You with all their heart, who have kept with Your servant, my father David, that which You have promised him; indeed, You have spoken with Your mouth and have fulfilled it with Your hand as it is this day. (1 Kings 8:23, 24)

God Establishes a Dynasty through David

When David approached God through Nathan about building a house for Him, God declared that He would build *David* a house and not the other way around. The meaning of this declaration was that God would establish a *dynasty* through David. This promise to David has come to be known as the Davidic Covenant. It is described this way in Psalm 89:3:

> I have made a covenant with My chosen;
> I have sworn to David My servant,
> I will establish your seed forever
> And build up your throne to all generations."

The Davidic Covenant

God reminds David in this covenant that it was He who took him from the pasture and following the sheep to be ruler over His people, Israel. The Lord was with him wherever he went, and He had defeated David's enemies all around him. God promised that He would make David a great name like the great men of the earth just as he had promised Abraham. Ever since the Lord had called Abraham, Moses, and Joshua, He had spoken forth His plan to bring His people into a land that He had promised them. To David He said that now He was going to appoint a place for His people, Israel, and plant them so that they would not be disturbed again. He goes on to say that He would set up a hereditary monarchy for the hHouse of David. When Saul sinned and rebelled against the Lord, he was set aside from the throne, and his descendants were cut off from succession. No king had ever been succeeded by his son in Israel. Now David knew that his son, Solomon, would succeed him. God also promised to discipline Solomon, and be a Father to him but not reject him or remove him from the throne as He had done to Saul.

God promised David that His lovingkindness would not depart from him or Solomon and that His house (or dynasty) would be established forever. What a revelation this must have been to David, especially since He understood the immense scope and import of covenant history so well! How awesome to think that his purpose in the unfolding of God's restoration of mankind had been planned by God from the very beginning. The establishment of a dynasty was crucially important because the lineage of David would go on forever, long after he died. David knew through this covenant that Jesus would come of his race! What joy that must have been! The Davidic Covenant in 2 Samuel 7:8–17 guaranteed that the family of David would always retain the right to rule Israel. The authority to rule from the throne would never pass to another family.

My covenant I will not violate,
nor will I alter the utterance of My lips.
Once I have sworn by My holiness,
I will not lie to David.
His descendants shall endure forever,
and his throne as the sun before Me.
It shall be established forever like the moon,
and the witness in the sky is faithful.
(Psalms 89:34–37)

David's dynasty ruled Judah for more than four hundred years. This was quite a contrast to the ruling families in the northern kingdom of Israel. It has been claimed that David's dynasty was longer in duration than any other single dynasty in the world! Of course, God's promise of a dynasty was one that lasted forever.

It is disappointing to discover that this dynasty of David apparently came to an end when Babylon conquered the nation of Israel, destroyed Jerusalem and the temple, and killed King Zedekiah and his sons. The Israelites were taken into exile in Babylon and removed from the beloved land. The kingly lineage of David was broken, and no descendant of David has occupied the throne since then. The prophet Jeremiah has this to say about the desolation of God's land, His city, and His people:

> Many nations will pass by this city, and they will say to one another, "Why has the Lord done thus to this great city?" Then they will answer, 'Because they forsook the covenant of the Lord their God and bowed down to other gods and served them. (Jeremiah 22:8, 9)

Thankfully God directed His prophets to speak truth into those empty and desolate years. Through Jeremiah, Isaiah, Ezekiel, Daniel, and others, a hope was given that their covenant God would fulfill His promises despite the unfaithfulness of His people.

> "Behold the days are coming," says the Lord, "that I will raise to David a Branch of righteousness; a King shall reign and prosper, and execute judgment and righteousness in the earth. In His days Judah will be saved, and Israel will dwell safely; now this is His name by which He will be called: THE LORD OUR RIGHTEOUSNESS." (Jeremiah 23:5–6)

Through Abraham and now through David, the promise of a Seed to be their King and Deliverer still stood strong because the promises in the covenant cannot fail! God had promised that the throne of David's kingdom would be established forever. This promise did not depend on an unbroken succession of rulers in David's dynasty, but it did establish the throne and the right to rule from his unbroken line of descent. The right to sit on the throne and rule the kingdom will never be transferred to another family. The promise of God cannot return void. "The Lord has sworn to David a truth from which He will not turn back; of the fruit of your body I will set upon your throne" (Psalm 132:11).

The Future Throne of David

The bottom line to all of these promises was that the man God sought to sit on the throne of David in the future had to be one who was loyal to God, one who was obedient, one who was faithful, one who could be trusted to rule justly over Israel and the kingdoms of this world. No man was able to fulfill these requirements. Only God Himself was worthy. Remember when God made the covenant with Abraham? He put Abraham to sleep, walked through the pieces of the slain animals, and consummated both ends of the covenant. God planned to do the same with the Davidic Covenant. The only King worthy to sit on David's throne was God Himself, and this necessitated that He become a man who was a literal Son of David from his lineage. God would complete both ends of His covenant with David.

With full assurance from the Word of God, we can believe that a descendant of David, the Seed of David, will sit on His throne in Israel because it is established forever. This King will come through the lineage of David, from the tribe of Judah, from the stump of Jesse. The Davidic Covenant flowed forth from the Abrahamic Covenant made so many years before, and just as David and Abraham believed God with an incredible, simple faith, so we can believe God with an incredible, simple faith. All of the covenants of God were fulfilled literally, and the Davidic Covenant will also be fulfilled literally when Jesus comes again. Jesus will return to literally sit on the throne of David and reign over a restored and reconciled earth. "The kingdom of the world has become the kingdom of our Lord and of His Christ, and He will reign for ever and ever" (Revelation 11:15).

As we marvel at the goodness of God and the time when He made this all-important covenant with David, we also are privileged to look into the humble heart of David when he responded to the words of the covenant.

> Who am I, O Lord God? And what is my house, that you have brought me this far? And yet this was a small thing in Your sight, O Lord God; and You have spoken of Your servant's house for a great while to come ... for your word's sake, and according to Your own heart, You have done all these great things, to make Your servant know them. Therefore You are great, O Lord God. For there is none like You, nor is there any God besides You, according to all that we have heard with our ears. (2 Samuel 7:18–20)

Although God's covenant with David was made with him personally, it is a revelation to all of us. We know that when Jesus returns to earth and fulfills this covenant, the Lord will triumph over all His enemies. When the high priest asked Jesus to tell them if He was the Christ, the Son of God, Jesus answered, "Hereafter you will see the Son of Man sitting at the right hand of Power, and coming on the clouds of Heaven" (Matthew 26:64).

In Psalms 110:1–2 (a psalm of David), we can see that David understood this.

> The Lord says to my Lord:
> Sit at My right hand
> until I make Your enemies a
> footstool for your feet.
> The Lord will stretch forth
> Your strong scepter from Zion, saying,
> Rule in the midst of Your enemies.

The curtain falls as David dies and is buried in the City of David. He dies with his son, Solomon, firmly established on his throne and with a promise of an everlasting throne firmly implanted in his heart.

From Stepping Stone to Stepping Stone

I saw a picture of a swiftly flowing river and knew that it was the River of Life. The width of the river and the strength of the current made it impossible to cross over to the other side without a boat or bridge or man-made device. Then I noticed wide, flat stepping stones bridging the gap from one shore to the other. They were interspersed in such a way that each one led to the next one and not one of them could be leapt over or considered unnecessary. I could see that they had been placed by a divine hand into a strategic plan or pathway and were leading to a destination on the opposite shore.

The Lord revealed to me that each stepping stone was a crucial and consequential link to the onward story of His covenant with creation and His progressive salvation plan to bring all mankind into reconciliation with Himself. The stepping stones were the covenants of God and represented the covenants with Adam, Noah, Abraham, Moses, Joshua, David, and finally Jesus Christ. I could see that no access to the New Covenant with Christ was possible without first traversing the Old Covenant stepping stones that led up to it. To leap from one Old Covenant stone to another and then stop abruptly before stepping onto the rock of the New Covenant would be pointless because I would not be able to get to the other side.

Instantaneously I knew that the course of His covenant was laid out before the beginning of time. It is the only truth, the only way to redemption, and is available to me, my family, and all men everywhere. As I watched the waters splashing and surging in the river, I realized that to venture out on this stepping-stone pathway required absolute commitment. It required conversion. It required a leap of faith. I couldn't imagine ever turning back. The Lord assured me that as I took His hand, He would keep my foot from slipping and lead me to the outer shore.

(HLC)

173

CHAPTER 15

FROM ALPHA TO OMEGA

When the Fullness of Time had Come

The curtain rises on a scene that takes place one thousand years after the time of David in the city of Nazareth in Galilee. An angel sent from God is speaking to a virgin named Mary. Gabriel says to her,

> Do not be afraid, Mary; for you have found favor with God. And behold, you will conceive in your womb and bear a son, and you shall name Him Jesus. He will be great and will be called the Son of the Most High; and the Lord God will give Him the throne of His father David; and He will reign over the house of Jacob forever, and His kingdom will have no end. (Luke 1:32, 33)

In this climactic culmination of the covenants of God, we are mindful of the exact timing of God's divine events on earth. The New International Version of the Bible begins this way in Galatians 4:4: "When the set time had fully come—" The following is from the American Standard Version:

> But when the fullness of time came, God sent forth His Son, born of a woman, born under the Law, so that He might redeem those who were under the Law, that we might receive the adoption as sons. (Galatians 4:4–5)

We see that God again called forth the One whom He had chosen to fulfill His purposes. In Hebrews 10:5, it is noted that when Jesus came into the world, He said, "Sacrifice and offering You have not desired, but a body You have prepared for Me." We marvel at the words of Psalm 139 when we contemplate that the Spirit of God formed the body of Jesus in His mother's womb:

> For You formed my inward parts; You wove me in my mother's womb. Your eyes have seen my unformed substance; and in Your book were all written the days that were ordained for me, when as yet there was not one of them. (Psalms 139: 13, 16)

This psalm offers deep affirmation to each one of us, but it is unthinkable when we consider that the Savior of the world, who had existed in the form of God, did not regard equality with God a thing to be grasped but emptied Himself, taking the form of a servant in that He became like men and was born a human being (Philippians 2:6, 7 AMP).

The events surrounding the birth of the Christ child are sensational in themselves, but when we realize that they fulfilled prophecies of the Old Testament given hundreds of years before, we can only conclude that all of God's promises come true! The Word of God from Isaiah 7:14 asserts that "the Lord Himself will give you a sign. Behold a virgin will be with child and bear a son, and she will call His name Immanuel." Fast-forwarding ahead 740 years, we find these words in Matthew 1:18, "Now the birth of Jesus Christ was as follows: When His mother, Mary, had been betrothed to Joseph, before they came together she was found to be with child by the Holy Spirit."

> Now all this took place to fulfill what was spoken by the Lord through the prophet: "Behold the virgin shall be with child

and shall bear a Son and they shall call His name Immanuel, which translated means, 'God with us." (Matthew 1:22)

If we allow ourselves to ponder the virgin birth of Jesus and His entrance into this world as a baby, we cannot help but be awed and astonished. Why hadn't He arrived on this planet in the same way that He departed? He left this earth by ascending into the clouds, so why didn't He arrive by descending from the clouds? His personage could have been illuminated with light, and He could have stood out from the crowd as tall, handsome, and charming. He could have appeared as a military leader dressed in the dazzling regalia of a soldier. Yet in Isaiah 53:2, He is referred to as "having no stately form or majesty, that we should look upon Him, nor appearance that we should be attracted to Him." The truth is that He humbled Himself and came to this earth to identify with us. The One who created the world became a helpless baby in a manger.

It is important to keep in mind that back in the day it was God who called Abraham out of Ur and said, "I will establish My covenant between Me and you and your descendants after you throughout their generations for an everlasting covenant" (Genesis 17:7). God chose Abraham and his descendants (the nation of Israel) as His very own. If you remember, God said that He had chosen the Israelites not because they were greater or more in number than any of the peoples but because He had set His love on them and kept the oath He had sworn to their forefathers.

Our God has revealed His plan for the redemption and restoration of mankind through the progressive stepping stones of the covenant. In Genesis 22:18, He promised to Abraham that "in your seed, all the nations of the earth shall be blessed." Jesus is the fulfillment of that promise. He is the Seed. We know how important and crucial genealogies, generations, and families are to our Creator. The Messiah, born in a manger in a Jewish nation, had to be of the Jewish race with Jewish parents, and He had to belong to a Jewish family. God had already identified His family by choosing and covenanting with the patriarchs of long ago, Abraham, Isaac, and Jacob, and then further narrowing His identity through Judah, Jesse, and David. The New Testament opens with this introduction: "The book of the genealogy of Jesus Christ, the son of David; the son of Abraham" (Matthew 1:1). After listing the male heads of all the generations from Abraham to Jacob, the introduction concludes with "and to Jacob was born Joseph the husband of Mary, by whom was born Jesus, who is called the Messiah" (Matthew 1:16).

Just as King David rejoiced in the revelation that God's promise of an everlasting dynasty meant that the Messiah would come from his lineage, now those who anticipated the fulfillment of the prophecies throughout the Old Testament rejoiced in the birth of the Son of God, who would sit on the throne of His father, David. When the priest Zacharias, the father of John the Baptist, heard of the impending birth of Jesus, he was filled with the Holy Spirit and rejoiced by saying,

> Blessed be the Lord God of Israel, for He has visited us and accomplished redemption for His people, and has raised up a horn of salvation for us in the house of David His servant— As He spoke by the mouth of His holy prophets from of old. (Luke 1:67)

God had desired from the beginning that Israel would be a model for the other nations and that through His provision and love the Israelites would exhibit what it was like to be in covenant with the living God. In fact, God had addressed the nation of Israel as His firstborn son (Exodus 4:22). His intention was for His people to be a light to all the idolatrous nations around them. Through the many years since the exodus from Egypt, this had not happened.

When Mary and Joseph brought the infant Jesus into the temple to be circumcised, a righteous and devout man named Simeon met them there. It had been revealed to Simeon that he would not die until he had seen the Lord's Christ. When Simeon saw Jesus, he took Him in his arms and blessed God, and filled with the Holy Spirit, he said, "For my eyes have seen your salvation, which you have prepared in the sight of all nations: A light for revelation to the Gentiles, and the glory of your people Israel" (Luke 2:32).

Jesus would be a "light to the Gentiles." The Scriptures tell us that the father and mother of Jesus marveled at the things that were being said about him (Luke 2:33). In His profound wisdom, God the Father chose the Savior of the world to be born into a human family, to be raised by a mother and father, and to be part of a larger arena of siblings and relatives. What better way could God convince us that families are of ultimate significance to Him? He designed them and chose them to carry out His divine plan of salvation and restoration! He magnifies the importance of the family, which is His masterpiece, through this particular Jewish family, as they adore their newborn in a rustic stable in a humble village called Bethlehem in the nation of Israel.

A Child?

When prophets foretold a prince would appear
to bring his glory and peace to the land;
the people rejoiced and looked for a man
to sit on the throne, a scepter in hand.

Some looked for a valiant victor of war,
with armies prepared to heed his command;
to strike fear in foes and scatter them wide
while reigning in power, a sword in his hand.

> *But who would have looked for a little child,*
> *whose coming kingdom they won't understand?*
> *A baby born to a family on earth,*
> *to be one of us, a scar in his hand?*
> *(HLC)*

This babe was sent to manifest and usher in the New Covenant, or as it is some-times called the "Messianic Covenant." The prophet, Jeremiah, prophesied this new covenant six hundred years before Jesus was born!

> Behold, days are coming, declares the Lord, when I will make a new covenant with the house of Israel and with the house of Judah, not like the covenant which I made with their fathers in the day I took them by the hand to bring them out of the land of Egypt, My covenant which they broke, although I was a husband to them, declares the Lord. "But this is the covenant which I will make with the house of Israel after those days," declares the Lord, "I will put My law within them and on their heart I will write it; and I will be their God, and they shall be My people." (Jeremiah 31:31)

Other passages in Scripture confirm this covenant, and this particular promise, which is given in Jeremiah 32:38–40, includes the children of God's covenant people.

> They shall be My people, and I will be their God and I will give them one heart and one way, that they may fear Me always, for their own good and for the good of their children after them. I will make an everlasting covenant with them that I will not turn away from them, to do them good; and I will put the fear of Me in their hearts so that they will not turn away from Me.

The Everlasting Covenant in Jesus the Christ

So Jesus came to this earth to inaugurate this New Covenant. It is imperative that we remember that a covenant had been made between God the Father and His Son, Jesus Christ, from all eternity. This *Everlasting Covenant* was transacted before the foundations of the world were laid. It preceded all the other covenants and is the "Alpha and Omega" of our long journey across the stepping stones of the covenant story. It is the basis upon which all the covenants have been made with man. In the divine wisdom of heaven, God foresaw even before creation that a covenant of redemption needed to be preordained. It became apparent that mankind would have neither the heart nor the power to obey His Law. How could the Holy have fellowship with the unholy? It was the desire of the Father's heart to reconcile the world to Himself and to have a relationship with His sons and daughters. Christ pledged Himself from eternity to come to earth to be the mediator of this new covenant. As God relentlessly pursued His covenants with Adam, Noah, Abraham, Israel (Moses), Joshua, and David, the Everlasting Covenant was undergirding each new motion to establish communion and union with mankind and to integrate the covenants into a planned and purposeful continuity. Because the Everlasting Covenant between the Father and the Son was ever in place, the progress of the covenants continued to move forward until the "fullness of time" came, when God sent forth His Son.

How can we know that this Everlasting Covenant between the Father and Jesus was in place before time began? As we search the Scriptures, we can find the answers to questions such as this. Peter refers to our redemption with the precious blood of Christ and goes on to say, "For He was foreknown before the foundation of the world, but has appeared in these last times for the sake of you" (1 Peter 1:19, 20). The Scriptures seem so clear in John 6:38, when Jesus says, "For I have come down from heaven, not to do my own will, but the will of Him who sent Me." These words of Jesus are a testimony to the love He has for the Father and the love the Father has for Him in the everlasting covenant:

> Father, I desire that they also, whom you have given Me, be with Me where I am, so that they may see My glory which You have given Me, for You loved Me before the foundation of the world. (John 17:24)

The outworking of the Everlasting Covenant from the Father to the Son is revealed through such passages as Isaiah 42:6, which says,

> I am the Lord, I have called you in righteousness, I will also hold you by the hand and watch over you, and I will appoint You as a covenant to the people, as a light to the nations.

Jesus and His Father had covenanted in heaven to redeem the world including the Gentiles. Jesus emptied Himself and came to earth in the form of a servant to actualize the covenant. He did not open His mouth as He endured the trials and persecution leading up to His crucifixion and was silent as a sheep before its shearers because He knew that His sufferings fulfilled the terms of the covenant He had made with His Father. All of this makes sense when we read a passage like this in Isaiah 53:6–8.

> All of us like sheep have gone astray, each of us has turned to his own way; but the Lord has caused the iniquity of us all to fall on Him. He was oppressed and He was afflicted, yet He did not open His mouth. Like a lamb that is led to the slaughter, and like a sheep that is silent before its shearers, He did not open His mouth.

It has already been stated that Jesus came to this earth to give His life as a ransom for many! The animal sacrifices in the Old

Covenant were offered year after year as a shadow of things to come. They reminded the people of their ongoing sins, and their inability to obey the law of God. The long course of the stepping stones leading up to this time of the coming of Christ is explained in Hebrews 10:5.

> Therefore, when He comes into the world, He says, "Sacrifice and offering You have not desired, but a body You have prepared for Me; in whole burnt offerings and sacrifices for sin you have taken no pleasure." Then I said "behold I have come (in the scroll of the book it is written of Me) to do Your will, O God."

Jesus often declared that He came to do His Father's will, to do nothing of His own initiative, and to speak only what the Father told Him to speak. In the Garden of Gethsemane He faced the ultimate test of submitting Himself to the Father's will. As He approached the garden, He knelt down and prayed, knowing that the humiliation and agony of the cross lay ahead. He prayed fervently, with sweat falling like drops of blood upon the ground. "Father, if You are willing, remove this cup from Me; yet not My will, but Yours be done" (Luke 22:41–42).

The Blood of the Covenant

All covenants are ratified by blood. It is not surprising then that blood was appropriated when Moses instituted the first covenant. After Moses had pronounced the laws, ordinances, and commandments to the people, "he took the blood of the calves and the goats, with water and scarlet wool and hyssop, and sprinkled both the book itself and the people, saying, 'This is the blood of the covenant which God commanded you'" (Hebrews 9:20). We, too, have the confidence that the New Covenant was instituted by blood, the blood of the Son of God.

Blood was essential to God because, as it says in Leviticus 17:11, "For the life of the flesh is in the blood, and I have given it to you upon the altar to make atonement for your souls; for it is the blood that makes atonement for your souls."

God is a Spirit and had no blood with which to enter into covenant with man, so He sent His only Son to take on our humanity in order to shed His blood in covenant. When Jesus came into the world, He said, "Sacrifice and offering You have not desired, but a body You have prepared for Me" (Hebrews 10:5). This transaction took place in eternity. As pointed out in 1 Peter 1:19, we were not redeemed with perishable things like silver or gold but with "precious blood as of a lamb unblemished and spotless, the blood of Christ. For He was foreknown before the foundation of the world, but has appeared in these last times for the sake of you."

The blood of Jesus surpassed all other blood in uniqueness and value because it was the blood of the one and only God-man.

The Memorial Meal

When the traditional Passover ritual was followed and the host served the lamb, one of the children would ask, "What is this?" The reply was, "This is the body of the lamb which our fathers ate in Egypt." It is recorded in Matthew 26:26–28 that when Jesus shared the Passover meal with His disciples, He broke the bread, blessed it, and said, "Take eat; this is My body." Next He took the cup, gave it to them, and said, "Drink from it all of you; for this is My blood of the covenant, which is poured out for many for forgiveness of sins." In Hebrews 9:22, these words are indelibly written for all time: "Without the shedding of blood there is no forgiveness of sin."

In the covenant at Sinai Moses sprinkled the blood of the sacrificial animals over the people, and in this way the Old Covenant was ratified. Jesus knew that His blood, soon to be poured out for all people, would commence and carry out the New Covenant. In this sacred supper with the disciples, Jesus did not sprinkle the wine on them or over them as Moses did. He gave the wine to them to drink and to swallow internally, commemorating the blood of the New Covenant. Earlier in the ministry of Jesus He had taught in the synagogue and said to his disciples,

> Truly, truly I say to you, unless you eat the flesh of the Son of Man and drink His blood, you have no life in yourselves. He who eats My flesh and drinks My blood abides in Me, and I in him. (John 6:53, 56)

At that time some of his disciples grumbled about this being a difficult statement and refused to listen to Him. Some of them left Him. Yet now as Jesus offered His body and blood in the memorial meal of the New Covenant, the disciples began to understand.

So Jesus ratified the New Covenant and instituted a memorial meal for us just as Moses had for the Israelites. Moses had instructed them,

> When your children say to you, "What does this rite mean to you?" you shall say, "it is a Passover sacrifice to the Lord who passed over the houses of the sons of Israel in Egypt when He smote the Egyptians, and spared our homes." And the people bowed low and worshiped. (Exodus 12:26)

What do we say to our children when we share this *new* memorial meal (the Lord's Supper, Holy Communion, the Eucharist) with them? Are we aware that the divine legacy of what Jesus did for us when He obeyed the Father's will and gave His body and blood for us depends on our passing on this truth from generation to generation? Let us not neglect the sharing of so great a truth with our children. Let us not take it for granted. Let us not become passive as to its importance, for it is a covenant meal! Let us together with our children and families "bow low and worship."

We have followed the trail of blood:

1. From the Garden of Eden when the Lord God made garments of animal skins for Adam and Eve
2. To Noah as he sacrificed clean animals on the altar after the flood
3. To the animal parts cut in half for the covenant ritual with Abraham
4. To the blood of the lambs applied over the lintels and doorposts of the Israelites at the time of the Exodus
5. To the sacrifices of animals for atonement in the Mosaic Covenant
6. To the animal sacrifices in the temple at the time of David and Solomon
7. To the precious blood of Jesus on the cross and the stream of blood running from His pierced side
8. To the memorial meal of the sacrament when we partake of His body and blood.

It was the will of the Father for Jesus to shed His blood once and for all (Hebrews 10:10) and thereby become God's Blood Covenant to mankind. "I will appoint You as a covenant to the people" (Isaiah 42:6).

What Happened at the Cross: Works of the Devil Destroyed

When we study the Scriptures to discover the purposes for which Jesus came in obedience to His Father's will, we cannot overlook the verse in 1 John 3:8, which is one of the most powerful statements of truth since the fall of man. "The Son of God appeared for this purpose, to destroy the works of the devil."

This transaction on the cross had been prophesied by God Himself in the Garden of Eden. In Genesis 3:15, He said to the serpent, "I will put enmity between you and the woman, and between your seed and her Seed; He shall bruise you on the head and you shall bruise him on the heel." This prophecy from the mouth of God was a covenant with Adam and with all the generations that followed. Uttered in the Garden of Eden, it came into fulfillment thousands of years later on the cross of Calvary! When Jesus foretold His death, He said, "Now judgment is upon this world; now the ruler of this world will be cast out" (John 12:31).

Jesus also destroyed the works of the devil by "having forgiven us all our transgressions, having cancelled out the certificate of debt consisting of decrees against us, which was hostile to us; and has taken it out of the way, having nailed it to the cross" (Colossians 2:13b–14).

What Happened at the Cross: Freedom from the Bondage and Curse of the Law

Jesus gives us a further explanation of His mission on this earth in Matthew 5:17, "Do not think that I came to abolish the Law or the Prophets; I did not come to abolish but to fulfill." We have seen many instances when His birth and life were astonishing fulfillments of prophecies in the Old Testament that were written hundreds of years before. Jesus also lived a sinless life and was therefore worthy to take our places on the cross and die in our stead. He fulfilled the Mosaic Law perfectly and redeemed mankind from the curse of the law, becoming a "curse for us" (Galatians 3:13).

The Lord had spoken through the prophet Jeremiah many years before, declaring that He would make a new covenant with His people. He promised, "I will put My law within them and on their heart I will write it; and I will be their God and they shall be My people" (Jeremiah 31:31).

When Jesus died on the cross, He defeated the Law of Sin and Death, which all men have inherited from Adam, and He fulfilled the Old Covenant with its Mosaic Laws and requirements. In the New Covenant we are granted the freedom of living by the "Law of the Spirit of Life." The death of Jesus releases our chains from slavery to sin and death, and His resurrection lifts us into the freedom of being led by the Holy Spirit! "Therefore there is now no condemnation for those who are in Christ Jesus. For the law of the Spirit of Life in Christ Jesus has set you free from the law of sin and of death" (Romans 8:2).

This revelation is enormous and far-reaching to all generations. Yet it can be difficult to understand that we are free when the evils of sin and death are ever-present in the world system and in our own flesh. Regardless, the Scriptures tell us the truth. On the cross Jesus set us free from the law of sin and death and set in motion a new law, a law that is written in our hearts. On the cross we were given new life and a new law that is worked out from within us. It is called the Spirit of Life in Christ Jesus. We are free to walk in victory by the ever-present power of the Holy Spirit and the new covenant written in our hearts! Amazing Grace! How can it be? We have the privilege of receiving this truth in faith and daily cooperating with the Holy Spirit to obey the law of the Spirit of Life.

"Where the Spirit of the Lord is, there is freedom" (2 Corinthians 3:17).

Our God has enacted a better covenant with us, but keep in mind that the law in the Old Covenant served its purpose of teaching us that we were sinful by nature and could not keep it on our own. The Law is good, which is why Jesus came not to abolish it but to obey it and fulfill it. Each stepping stone has led us forward and is essential to complete the purposes of a Father, whose goal has always been to restore and reconcile the world to Himself.

It was the will of the Father for Jesus to obey and fulfill the Law, to become a *curse* for us, to defeat the Law of Sin and Death, and then to graciously provide the Law of the Spirit of Life in Christ Jesus to live by forever. What a Father! What a Savior! What a Holy Spirit!

What Happened at the Cross: One New Man

In studying the covenants of God, we realize that the nation of Israel, the Jews, are God's chosen people. Yet God's covenant with Abraham included this promise: "And in you all the families of the earth will be blessed" (Genesis 12:3).

We have learned that God's heart desired the Gentiles to be included in His salvation plan. Jesus revealed that He and His Father were one when He said, "I have other sheep, which are not of this fold; I must bring them also, and they will hear My voice; and they will become one flock with one shepherd" (John 10:16).

How did Jesus accomplish uniting the Jews and Gentiles into one flock? The answer is found in Ephesians 2:12–16, as Paul addresses the Gentiles,

> Remember that you were at that time separate from Christ, excluded from the commonwealth of Israel, and strangers to the covenants of promise, having no hope and without God in the world. But now in Christ Jesus you who formerly were far off have been brought near by the blood of Christ. For He Himself is our peace, who made both groups into one and

broke down the barrier of the dividing wall, by abolishing in His flesh the enmity, which is the Law of commandments contained in ordinances, so that in Himself He might make the two into one new man, thus establishing peace, and might reconcile them both in one body to God through the *cross*, by it having put to death the enmity.

This is very good news! At one time the Gentiles could not receive the blessings of the covenants unless they submitted to the Mosaic Law, underwent circumcision, and obeyed the Jewish ordinances. When Jesus died, that Mosaic wall, the middle wall, was broken down. Through the cross, Christ has reconciled both groups into one new man to God. Hallelujah!

When Jesus bowed His head and gave up His spirit on the cross, the Gospel of John records His last word, which was *"tetelestai!"* Our Bibles translate that word into three words meaning "It is finished!" (John 19:30). To the Jews and Romans this word would have meant that a "debt was paid in full." As we have considered the exponential and eternal meaning of the blood of Jesus and His suffering and death on the cross, we can well understand His cry of completion in paying in full for the sins of mankind. Now sons and daughters could be reconciled to the Father again because the sin of separation had been removed once and for all. Yet when we attempt to plummet to the end of everything that Jesus accomplished on the cross, we become aware that we can never come to the end of it. It is fathomless. It is limitless. The depth of the word *tetelestai* is very deep indeed!

Father God in Covenant

We have been immersed in the mind-stretching, spirit-stretching wonders of the New Covenant made between God the Father, His Son, Jesus Christ, and the Holy Spirit. So far we have focused our attention on the covenantal acts of Jesus on earth, but at the end of

His suffering on the cross, He cried out with a loud voice, "Father, into Your hands I commit My spirit" (Luke 23:46). When Jesus died, the attention begins to focus on the Father's role in the Holy Covenant. The spotlight moves to the resurrection of Jesus and the question "Who raised Jesus from the dead?". In Peter's sermon on the day of Pentecost, He declared,

> This Man, delivered over by the predetermined plan and foreknowledge of God, you nailed to a cross by the hands of godless men and put Him to death. But God raised Him up again, putting an end to the agony of death, since it was impossible for Him to be held in its power. (Acts 2:23, 24)

Another reference to the Father raising Jesus from the dead is recorded in Acts 13:32 when Paul says,

> And we preach to you the good news of the promise made to the fathers, that God has fulfilled this promise to our children in that He raised up Jesus, as it is also written in the second Psalm, "You are My Son; today I have begotten You." As for the fact that He raised Him up from the dead, no longer to return to decay, He has spoken in this way: "I will give you the holy and sure blessings of David."

In Acts 13:37, Paul says, "He whom God raised did not undergo decay."

The covenantal relationship between the Father and Son is evident. If the Father had not raised the Son from the dead, it would mean that Christ's sacrifice was insufficient. The sacrifice of Jesus on the cross was accepted by the Father as atonement for our sins! If Christ had not been raised by the Father, our faith would be worthless, and we would still be in our sins (1 Corinthians 15:17). It is a tremendous truth to know that Jesus, our Lord, is alive! Jesus appeared to John on the island of Patmos (sixty years after His death) and said, "I am the first and the last, and the living One; and I was dead, and behold, I am alive forevermore" (Revelation 1:17–18).

To the people of Athens, Paul preached that God was calling people everywhere to repent because He had fixed a day in which He will judge the world in righteousness through Jesus, whom He had appointed and through whom God had provided proof to all men by raising Him from the dead (Acts 17:30–31). The resurrection of Jesus also proves that God has the power to raise all men from the dead.

As these high and lofty occurrences in the spiritual and earthly realms swirl around in our minds and settle for a moment in our consciousness, we can conclude that the mystery of salvation includes both the death of Christ and the resurrection of Christ. In Romans 6:4, Paul says that "we have been buried with Him through baptism into death, so that as Christ was raised from the dead through the glory of the Father, so we too might walk in newness of life."

Through the working of God the Father's strength, "He raised Jesus from the dead and seated Him at His right hand in the heavenly places, far above all rule and authority and power and dominion, and every name that is named, not only in this age but also in the one to come" (Ephesians 1:20, 21). Our glorious God of mercy also gave us this promise:

> But God, being rich in mercy, because of His great love with which He loved us, even when we were dead in our transgressions, made us alive together with Christ (by grace you have been saved), and raised us up with Him, and seated us with Him in the heavenly places in Christ Jesus. (Ephesians 2:4–6)

These spectacular provisions happened because of the great love of the Father from all eternity, and now the delight of His heart is to have a relationship with His sons and daughters. This truth is found in Romans 8:15. "You have received a spirit of adoption as sons by which we cry out, 'Abba! Father!' The Spirit Himself testifies with our spirit that we are children of God."

It is my prayer that you will acknowledge the hunger within you to experience the Father's love. No other earthly pursuit will satisfy your hunger. The Word of the Lord came to Jeremiah and said, "Before I formed you in the womb I knew you" (Jeremiah 1:4). That is how intimately He knows you and loves you. Jesus cleared the way for you to reach out to God and cry out, "Abba! Father!" The Father is waiting.

The Sign of the New Covenant: The Holy Spirit

The sign and seal of the Everlasting Covenant and therefore the New Covenant, is the Holy Spirit. The Holy Spirit is not a passive member of the Trinity and has been active in all the covenants leading up to the New Covenant.

When Jesus reached manhood, He came to the Jordan, where John was baptizing. When John saw Jesus coming to him, He said, "Behold, the Lamb of God Who takes away the sin of the world!" Then John testified, saying,

> I have seen the Spirit descending as a dove out of heaven, and He remained upon Him. John said that he had been told that "He upon whom you see the Spirit descending and remaining upon Him, He is the One who baptizes in the Holy Spirit. I myself have seen, and have testified that this is the Son of God. (John 1:32, 33)

We are told that Jesus, who was full of the Holy Spirit, was led around in the wilderness by the Spirit for forty days to be tempted by the devil. He then returned to Galilee in the power of the Spirit and began His ministry. Later when Peter addressed the Gentiles, he preached about Jesus to them. He proclaimed,

> You know of Jesus of Nazareth, how God anointed Him with the Holy Spirit and with power, and how He went about doing good and healing all who were oppressed by the devil, for God was with Him. (Acts 10:38)

Jesus went about preaching and teaching the kingdom of God in the power of the Holy Spirit. Jesus had come to do the will of the Father and to teach what the Father gave Him to teach. In John 8:25, Jesus said to the Jews,

> He who sent Me is true; and the things which I heard from Him, these I speak to the world. When you lift up the Son of Man, then you will know that I am He, and I do nothing of My own initiative, but I speak these things as the Father taught Me. And He who sent Me is with Me; he has not left Me alone, for I always do the things that are pleasing to Him.

With this in mind, we read these words of Jesus in Luke 4:43: "I must preach the kingdom of God in other cities also; for I was sent for this purpose." Jesus went about not only preaching the kingdom of God but also *doing* the kingdom of God. The disciples were with Him when He opened the eyes of the blind, restored hearing to deaf ears, raised the dead, healed the sick, performed miracles, cast out demons, and took authority over the forces of nature. He was anointed by the Holy Spirit.

For the three and a half years that Jesus ministered on this earth, He taught and demonstrated the kingdom of God. He had declared that this was one of the purposes for which He was sent. We always need to remember that He went about under the anointing of the Holy Spirit. He knew, and we know that the power of the Holy Spirit is absolutely essential to the outworking of the kingdom of God.

The Holy Spirit in Us

Before the death of Jesus, He had spoken to His disciples, telling them that He was returning to the Father, who had sent Him. He knew that they were saddened by the prospect of His leaving, but He consoled them by telling them that it was to their advantage for Him to go away so that they would receive the Holy Spirit.

> For if I do not go away, the Helper will not come to you, but if I go, I will send Him to you ... But when He comes He will guide you into all the truth; for He will not speak on His own initiative, but whatever He hears, He will speak and He will disclose to you what is to come. (John 16:7, 13)

The Father's hand was in all that happened with the Son both before and after the crucifixion. In Acts 1:4, we are told that before Jesus ascended into heaven, He gathered His apostles together and commanded them not to leave Jerusalem but to wait for what the Father had promised, "which you have heard of from Me; for John baptized with water, but you will be baptized with the Holy Spirit not many days from now" (Acts 1:4). Again the Father had a major role in giving to the world the gift of the Holy Spirit as our sign of the New Covenant. Already sanctioned in the everlasting covenant of the Trinity in heaven, Jesus would send the Holy Spirit to His disciples (from the Father) to carry out the work of the kingdom. In John, He said,

> I will ask the Father, and He will give you another Helper, that He will be with you forever; that is the Spirit of truth,

whom the world cannot receive, because it does not see Him or know Him, but you know Him, because He abides with you and will be with you. (John 14:16)

Jesus also said, "The Helper, the Holy Spirit, whom the Father will send in My name, He will teach you all things, and bring to your remembrance all that I said to you" (John 14:26).

In the second chapter of Acts, Peter says to the people, "Repent, and each of you be baptized in the name of Jesus Christ for the forgiveness of your sins; and you will receive the gift of the Holy Spirit. For the promise is for you and your children and for all who are far off, as many as the Lord our God will call to Himself." So the Holy Spirit was poured out on the day of Pentecost. If this Scripture had not been recorded for us, we would be tempted to believe that the Baptism of the Holy Spirit was a gift and provision for that generation only and not available to us and our children. Peter recorded the simple truth that this promise was not only for them at that time and for their children but also for "all who are far off!" That would be us.

Ambassadors for Christ

After His resurrection Jesus appeared to His chosen apostles over a period of forty days and spoke to them of the things that had to do with the kingdom of God.

He called the twelve together, and gave them power and authority over all the demons and to heal diseases. And He sent them out to proclaim the kingdom of God and to perform healing. (Luke 9:1–2)

Those of us who have inhabited the earth since the time of Jesus are to proclaim the kingdom of God, which is here, at hand, and is coming in more fullness in the future, by actively teaching what Jesus taught and doing what Jesus did. Are we engaged in the daily pursuit of being filled with the knowledge of His will, walking worthy of our calling, and proclaiming the kingdom of God to those whom God gives to us? Is this our daily prayer, "Thy kingdom come, Thy will be done on earth as it is in heaven?" The burning desire of our hearts should be to demonstrate the lifestyle of Jesus under the anointing of the Holy Spirit so that those in our sphere of influence will witness the righteousness, joy, and peace that God intended us to have from the beginning. As Jesus prepares to come again to rule the earth, we need to prepare the people of His kingdom to receive Him! The prophet Malachi asked the question, "But who can endure the day of His coming? And who can stand when He appears?" (Malachi 3:2).

Do you recall the covenant that God made with David when He said, "Your house and your kingdom shall endure before Me forever; Your throne shall be established forever" (2 Samuel 7:16)? After David's death the prophets continued to prophesy that a descendant of David would appear and establish a kingdom from Jerusalem. This kingdom would grow and fill the earth with the government of God. The prophet Isaiah said,

> For unto us a Child is born, unto us a Son is given, and the government will be upon His shoulder and His name will be called Wonderful, Counselor, Mighty God, Everlasting Father, Prince of Peace. Of the increase of His government and peace there will be no end, upon the throne of David and over His kingdom. (Isaiah 9:6, 7)

When the angel foretold the birth of Jesus to Mary, He said, "The Lord God will give Him the throne of His father, David, and He will reign over the house of Jacob forever, and His kingdom will have no end" (Luke 1:32, 33). When Jesus returns, His kingdom will expand to include all the nations of the world.

Now we have made our way across the stepping stones of the covenants of God. We have followed the covenants with the understanding that each stepping stone brought us closer to the grand goal of God the Father, reconciling us to Himself. Our Covenant God announces the most awesome news of the ages in 2 Corinthians 6: 16, 18, which says,

> "I will dwell in them and walk among them;
> and I will be their God,
> and they shall be My people.

> And I will be a father to you,
> and you shall be sons and
> daughters to Me."
> says the Lord Almighty.

Paul sums it all up in this passage in 2 Corinthians.

> Therefore if anyone is in Christ, he is a new creature; the old things passed away; behold, new things have come. Now all these things are from God, who reconciled us to Himself through Christ and gave us the ministry of reconciliation, namely, that God was in Christ reconciling the world to Himself, not counting their trespasses against them, and He has committed to us the word of reconciliation. (2 Corinthians 5:17–20)

Consider the following passage as well: "Therefore, we are ambassadors for Christ, as though God were making an appeal through us" (2 Corinthians 5:20).

The curtain has not fallen on the scene of Jesus on the cross or the empty tomb or Jesus ascending into heaven or the day of Pentecost. It will not fall, as we stand today on the last stepping stone of the covenants, preaching the kingdom, and appealing as ambassadors for Christ, "You are reconciled to God!"

In the meantime, we wait for His return.

CHAPTER 16

FROM PROMISE TO PROMISE

After we have traversed the river of life over the stepping stones of the covenants that God has provided for mankind from the time of Adam and Eve until the present day, we can be absolutely sure of two things. One thing is that God always keeps His promises. In fact, when King Solomon dedicated the temple in Jerusalem, he declared that "not one word has failed of all His good promises" (1 Kings 8:56). This proclamation resounds through the centuries. Another certain thing is that from eternity God has chosen to carry out His plan for creation and the subsequent restoration through families. His motivation was and is love!

From the beginning God revealed Himself as a Father and made it clear that He desired a relationship with His people. He loved us unconditionally and longed for many sons and daughters who would love Him in return. He intended to accomplish this by creating a *Family Covenant* on earth, one that would mirror the intimacy shared by the Father, Son, and Holy Spirit in heaven in unending joy and inexpressible love. He did not scatter his people around here and there as solitary individuals but benevolently placed them in families with the express purpose of raising the children to know Him and love Him. In this passage from Ephesians 3:14–19, Paul gives us an idea of what our family God has in mind for our families, who are in covenant with Him.

For this reason I bow my knees before the Father from whom every family in heaven and on earth derives its name, that He would grant you, according to the riches of His glory, to be strengthened with power through His Spirit in the inner man, so that Christ may dwell in your hearts through faith; and that you, being rooted and grounded in love, may be able to comprehend with all the saints what is the breadth and length and height and depth, and to know the love of Christ which surpasses knowledge, that you may be filled up to all the fullness of God.

Our Father opens His hand and gives grace and blessing to the families on this earth who respond to the offer of His family covenant. It is God the Father who initiates every covenant He has ever made with mankind, and it is no different with the family covenant. It is His idea and can only be actualized by the revelation of His Word, the inward work of the Holy Spirit, and our response in faith. Surely it should be our eternal hope to hold our families before God and receive beautiful promises like those in Isaiah 44:3.

> For I will pour out water on the thirsty land
> And streams on the dry ground;
> I will pour out My Spirit on your offspring,
> And My blessing on your descendants

How can we as family covenant keepers respond to such grace as this? We know that the success of establishing a covenant household depends on the grace of God, but how do we participate in God's plan? How do we influence our children and grandchildren, our parents and siblings, our nieces and nephews, our cousins, our uncles and aunts, and all who belong to them to believe in the living God and walk in covenant with Him?

But the lovingkindness of the Lord is from everlasting to everlasting on those who revere Him, and His righteousness to children's children, to those who keep His covenant, and remember His precepts to do them. (Psalms 103:17–18)

On the basis of this psalm we can immediately see that it is of the utmost importance for our children to first witness the reverence we have for our Father in heaven. In order to train our children to be obedient to the Word of God, we first must "remember His precepts to do them." We cannot raise covenant keepers if *we* are not covenant keepers. You might recall that when God made a covenant with Abraham, He said, "For I have known him, in order that he may command his children and his household after him, that they keep the way of the Lord, to do righteousness and justice" (Genesis 18:19). It is our assignment, our privilege not to be deferred, to transmit to our children the unconditional love of their Covenant Creator, who loved them before they were even born and wove them together in their mother's womb. As we receive this assignment to train and enfold our children and the generations after us in the everlasting covenant of God, we can trust that the Holy Spirit will pour out His lovingkindness through us so that streams of living waters will flow far beyond our lifetime.

As parents and grandparents, we respond to the wonderful promises given through the family covenant of God by aligning our households with the precepts of God and teaching our children the Word of God. By so doing they will learn for themselves that Jesus is the Way, the Truth, and the Life.

Hear, O Israel! The Lord is our God, the Lord is One! You shall love the Lord your God with all your heart and with all your soul and with all your might. These words, which I am commanding you today, shall be on your heart. You shall teach them diligently to your sons and shall talk of them when you sit in your house and when you walk by the way and when you lie down and when you rise up. You shall bind them as a sign on your hand and they shall be as frontals on your forehead. You shall write them on the doorposts of your house and on your gates. (Deuteronomy 6:4–9)

Another important aspect of upholding the family covenant should be to pass along our testimony of the power of the blood of Jesus. The story of the Passover in Exodus is a graphic foreshadowing of the efficacy of the blood of Jesus, which was shed once and for all and for all time. To review this biblical account in Exodus, the heads of the Israelite households were instructed to take "a lamb for a house." Further instructions were to slay the lamb, dip a bunch of hyssop in the blood, and apply some of the blood to the lintel and doorposts of the house. None of the family members were to go outside the door until morning so that the whole family was "under the blood." The Lord promised that when He saw the blood, it would be a sign of faith for Him to pass over, not allowing the Destroyer to come in to smite the firstborn. God chose to call forth families and households, as He delivered the children of Israel out of Egyptian bondage.

The Jewish father had the privilege of knowing that what he had done by applying the blood was in obedience to God for the saving of his family as well as himself. The Lord commanded the people of Israel to observe this event of the Passover as an ordinance for them and for their children forever. He told them to be ready with an answer when their children asked about the meaning of this rite in the future.

The Scriptures declare that Christ our Passover has also been sacrificed (1 Corinthians 5:7). He is "a Lamb for a House," and we have the privilege of applying the blood of Jesus by faith over our households. The trail of blood, the scarlet cord, that has meandered through the story of salvation from the time of Adam and Eve to the blood of Jesus on the cross has continued to flow to the present day. We are not redeemed with perishable things like silver and gold but with precious blood as of a lamb unblemished and spotless, the blood of Christ (1 Peter 1:18, 19). Not only should we place our loved ones "under the blood" each day in protection from the evil one, but we also should be ready with an answer when they ask the meaning of the blood of Jesus and what it has meant to us personally.

In faith, we can verbally place the blood of Jesus over the heads of each of our children and over the doors and roofs of our homes. Many walk a bloodline of Jesus around their homes and lands, their places of business, their schools and classrooms. When a family member is undergoing an assault of the enemy, we can apply the blood of Jesus over that situation. In the book of Revelation, John refers to the "accuser of our brethren" as being thrown down and says that the saints overcame him because of the blood of the Lamb and because of the word of their testimony (Revelation 12:11). There is power in the blood of Jesus!

At the beginning of this book we considered the choice that was put before Adam and Eve and the decision that they made. With long, long hindsight we can now gain a perspective of God's heart, which was always to share His covenant love with sons and daughters, whom He had created in His image. At the same time we observe that God created man with free will. Because they listened to the lie of the serpent, Adam and Eve chose to make their own way, to break the covenant of union with God, and to declare their independence. How can we "reverse the tape" and return to dependence and union with our God? We have the advantage of looking back on history and observing the empty deceitfulness of sin and the futile failure of mankind to live life on their own. As we stand hand in hand with our families, we, too, have a choice to make. God has provided a doorway through which we can once again step into union with Him. The doorway is water baptism.

The New Testament believers were presented with a radical gospel, which required that they make a U-turn, give up all of their old ways of life, and choose the kingdom of God with absolute dependence on the Father just like Jesus.

> Then Peter said to them, "Repent, and let every one of you be baptized in the name of Jesus Christ for the remission of sins, and you shall receive the gift of the Holy Spirit. For the promise is to you and to your children, and to all who are afar off, as many as the Lord your God will call." Then those who gladly received his word were baptized; and that day about three thousand souls were added to them. (Acts 2:38–41)

Whereas baptism is a declaration of faith and a doorway to dependence on the Father for us, it is so much more than that. As we enter the waters of baptism, we enter the death of Christ, and when we rise up from the waters, we are united in His resurrection into newness of life. Paul says this in Romans 6:3–4:

> Or do you not know that all of us who have been baptized into Christ Jesus have been baptized into His death? Therefore we have been buried with Him through baptism into death, so that as Christ was raised from the dead through the glory of the Father, so we too might walk in newness of life.

How important it is to live as testimonies to our families, having been baptized into the death of Jesus and raised up into newness of life in Him! One of our missions in the kingdom of God is to demonstrate to our children that our old nature is diminishing day by day and the spirit of this world is fading away. In 2 Corinthians 3:3, Paul says, "You are a letter of Christ, cared for by us, written not with ink but with the Spirit of the living God, not on tablets of stone but on tablets of human hearts."

Our children and wider family of relatives (which may include unsaved parents and grandparents) should be able to observe by our examples the reality of the newness of life and the power of the resurrection, which God promised to us when He raised Christ from the dead. The promises of God never fail.

When Jesus came up out of the waters after He was baptized by John, the Father's voice spoke out of the heavens, "This is My beloved Son, in whom I am well-pleased" (Matthew 3:17). When each one of our family members comes up out of the waters of baptism, I believe the Father in heaven is well-pleased. Each one has become His heart's desire, His son or daughter.

We become radicalized through baptism. It is the antithesis of independence and self-reliance, and it is the way it should have been from the beginning. May our covenant households embrace this truth!

As we seek to construct a covenant household, a major foundation stone is for us to cultivate time alone with our God, to worship Him, to make our requests known to Him, and to hear His instructions. The inspiring story of Cornelius is found in Acts 10, and it illustrates what can happen when the heads of households seek God daily in faith and intimacy. The Bible informs us that Cornelius was a Roman centurion who lived in Caesarea and believed in the God of Israel along with his household. He was a devout man who prayed to God continually. One day in a vision he saw an angel of the Lord who said that he should dispatch some men to Joppa and send for a man named Simon, who was also called Peter, "and he will speak words to you by which you will be saved, you and all your household" (Acts 11:14). After Cornelius had sent the men, he gathered his family and close friends together in his house and waited. When Peter arrived with some of his men, he began to tell them about Jesus and all that He had done. He went on to tell them about Jesus' death on the cross and how God raised Him up on the third day. He personally testified to eating and drinking with Jesus after His resurrection and witnessed to them that through His name everyone who believes in Him receives forgiveness of sins. While Peter was still speaking, the Holy Spirit fell on all those who were listening to the message. Everyone was amazed because the Holy Spirit had been poured out on the Gentiles as well! They heard them speaking in tongues and praising God. Peter said, "Surely no one can refuse the water for these to be baptized who have received the Holy Spirit, just as we, can he?" (Acts 10:47).

What an incredible blessing this was for Cornelius and his family! Because he was a man of prayer and heard and obeyed the Word God sent to him through the angel, he and his whole family were saved, and it became public knowledge that the Gentiles had received the same gift of the Holy Spirit as the Jews had received on the day of Pentecost! The Gentiles were now included in the Family Covenant! Are we willing to spend private, intimate time alone with God on behalf of our families? God may not send an angel to us, but He always answers our prayers. In 1 Kings 19:11–13, Elijah stood on a mountainside and sought the Lord in his despair. He listened for God's voice in a strong wind, in an earthquake, and in a fire but finally heard it in a sound of gentle blowing—a still, small voice. As we wait on the Lord for answers in regard to our families, He will answer us in a way of His choosing, in an inner intuition through the Word of God or through other believers who bring us a message, such as Peter did. The key is spending time with Him, pouring out our hearts in intercession, and believing that He will answer.

Our family God has honored and memorialized the name of Cornelius through all these years to prompt us to pray and prevail for our families. We need to wait in expectancy and be willing to obey the voice of the Lord through action.

Another major building block in the construction of the household of faith or the Family Covenant is to believe that God desires whole households to be saved. When we look at the trend in America to raise our children to be independent and choose for themselves whom they will serve, when we watch our children being snatched away by the lure of this world and its ambitions, when we stand back and lament the evils of the addictions that have attached themselves to our children, it is a temptation to throw up our arms in helplessness and feel powerless to do anything about it!

It is incredulous that the church has stood by, while the devil has marched on, corrupting our families and our nation. He has achieved this by deceiving the heads of families into believing that they are saved but have no power to influence their children. Of course, we have no power to "make them believe," but we do have the power of prayer to ask God, who knew them from before they were born, to fulfill His plan for each of them. These beautiful words are written in Psalm 139:16: "In Your book were all written the days that were ordained for me, when as yet there was not one of them." When we pray for our children and all who belong to us, the words of the psalmist resound in our ears, "The Lord will accomplish what concerns me; Your lovingkindness, O Lord, is everlasting; Do not forsake the works of Your hands" (Psalm 138:8). God listens to us when we listen to Him.

As we partake in the family covenant, we have the responsibility of praying for our family members, trusting that our Covenant God will answer. As we marvel at the faithfulness of God and His lovingkindness through all the covenants in the Bible, we know without a doubt that He keeps all of His promises. This covenant promise of saving our families is no exception. It is God's will that our whole family be saved, and He asks us to ask and to believe that God will accomplish this in His own time and in His own way.

We tend to forget that marriage and family was God's idea in the first place, and the distorted picture we have of families in the present day is due to the fact that men and women have taken marriage and family into their own hands and redesigned it or manipulated it to suit their own thinking and desires. They call it the "modern family."

Without the awareness that God desires to save whole households, it is possible to overlook the portions of Scripture that depict this as truth. When God saved Noah and all his house in the ark, he included his three daughters-in-law. When God called Abraham and made a covenant with him, He told him that he and his whole household were to be circumcised. God established His covenant not only with Abraham but with his descendants and the generations after him. We have already claimed the illustration of the Passover in Exodus, where God chose to save Israel by families. The lamb was for the whole house. Rahab will always be a beacon of light as a woman who cared not only for her own salvation but for that of her extended family—her father, mother, brothers, sisters, and all who belonged to them. These are just a few examples of God's heart to save whole families.

It is evident that in the Old Testament people were saved household by household. It is the same in the New Testament. We have already read the amazing story of Cornelius in Acts 10. Another inspiring story is found in Acts 16. It is about the jailer at Philippi, and it has become a standard bearer for all the other verses in the New Testament that deal with the salvation of families. When the jailer at Philippi asked Paul and Silas what he must do to be saved, they said, "Believe in the Lord Jesus, and you will be saved, you and your household" (Acts 16:31).

It is important to note that this salvation doesn't happen automatically to all of them at once just because the head of the house believed. The Word goes on to say that Paul and Silas spoke the Word of the Lord to him together with all who were in his house. In addition to this, the jailer underwent a change in his behavior and attitude since he washed the wounds of Paul and Silas and put food before them. His family must have witnessed this transformation. It was the power of the Word of God preached to all of them and the testimony of the father that ignited faith in each of them. Subsequently "the jailer was baptized, with all his household. He later rejoiced greatly, having believed in God with his whole household" (Acts 16:33, 34).

This is true also of other accounts in the gospel. Some of you might be familiar with the testimony of the nobleman who implored Jesus to come to Capernaum to heal his son because he was at the point of death. Jesus replied to him, "Go, your son lives" (John 4:49). The man believed the word that Jesus had spoken to him and later discovered that at that very hour his son had recovered and had not died. Not only did this nobleman believe, but his whole household believed because of this miracle of healing by Jesus.

The apostle Paul appears larger than life in the pages of Acts and in his epistles to the churches. It comes as somewhat of a surprise when we read in Acts 23:16 that when Paul was in Jerusalem and was about to be brought before the council, the son of Paul's sister heard of a plot to kill Paul through an ambush. A conspiracy of more than forty Jews had taken an oath to neither eat nor drink until they had killed Paul. Paul's nephew entered the barracks to tell Paul and was then led to the commander to inform him of the plan. This act by Paul's nephew saved his life! It also saved much of the revealed truth that is ours through Paul's teachings. In his epistles Paul often refers to his kinsmen (male relatives). An example is found in Romans 16:7, which says, "Greet Andronicus and Junias, my kinsmen and my fellow prisoners, who are outstanding among the apostles, who also were in Christ before me."

When the Triune God created man in His image, both male and female, he blessed them and commanded them to "be fruitful and multiply." Certainly the Lord foreknew that if a husband and wife walked as one with Him and with each other, they would not be content until their children, who are part of both of them, would be in covenant as well! God is a mastermind of creation, and the family covenant dominated the desires in His heart and mind from the beginning. Likewise, when older children have received Jesus as their Savior, they are zealous to bring their unbelieving parents, siblings, cousins, and all who belong to them to a knowledge of the truth about the Covenant God. Nobody on earth can care as much as family members for the salvation of one another because they are part of one another.

The bonding of love among family members is eternal and spiritual. Even among families who may not be aware that God Almighty created them and gave them to one another, the strength of love and loyalty is evident. It is intrinsic and inborn. One touching scene from the Bible evokes this passion of family love, which our Lord Jesus Christ experienced on the cross. Mary, the mother of Jesus, was standing before Him as He was dying. John 19:26–27 describes this moment to us.

> When Jesus saw His mother, and the disciple whom He loved standing nearby, He said to His mother, "Woman, behold your son!" Then He said to the disciple, "Behold, your mother." From that hour the disciple took her into his own household.

Our family God has revealed that His desire is to save whole families. Yet through the years this emphasis has been somewhat overlooked in the church, and it seems as if evangelists focus more on one-by-one conversions. It is up to us not only to travail in prayer for our unsaved family members but also to teach and encourage others in the Body of Christ to do the same. This is part of the Family Covenant. When we pray, believing, He has promised to save our family. He has said, "Believe on the Lord Jesus Christ and you will be saved, you and your household" (Acts 16:31).

As we pray, we need to keep a few essential truths in mind. The first obstacle to our prayer is that the god of this world has blinded the minds of the unbelieving so that they might not see the light of the gospel (2 Corinthians 4:4). When Adam and Eve sinned, they forfeited their authority to the evil one or the "god of this world." When Christ died, He reclaimed that authority and gave it to us. "He called the twelve together, and gave them power and authority over all the demons and to heal diseases. And He sent them out to proclaim the kingdom of God and to perform healing" (Luke 9:1).

Because of our God-given authority, we can ask God to save our families. Do we really understand that our prayers, based on God's covenant promises for our children, will be answered because He has bound Himself to the words of His mouth? The truth is that it is beyond our understanding and requires our faith. Faith activates the covenant! If we feel as if we don't have enough faith to believe for the salvation and righteousness of our children and our parents and siblings, then we can ask Him for a strengthening of our faith—the faith with which we believed for our own salvation.

We have the authority to command the scales of unbelief to fall from the eyes of our family members. The Bible reminds us that we were once like this, and now we can ask God to rescue our children and loved ones from this present darkness:

> And you were dead in your trespasses and sins, in which you formerly walked according to the course of this world, according to the prince of the power of the air, of the spirit that is now working in the sons of disobedience. Among

them we too all formerly lived in the lusts of our flesh, indulging the desires of the flesh and of the mind, and were by nature, children of wrath, even as the rest. (Ephesians 2:2)

On the basis of the finished work of Jesus in the new covenant, we can command Satan to take His hands off our children's minds and eyes so that they can see the light of the gospel. We should always be mindful that we are not fighting against flesh and blood but against rulers and forces of darkness (Ephesians 6:12). Because we know that Christ defeated the power of the devil on the cross and gave us the authority to fight, we can be assured that we are more than conquerors in the kingdom.

As fathers, mothers, and grandparents, we should also be concerned about our children and grandchildren's *earthly* salvation right now, as well as their *eternal* salvation. Some sit back and breathe a sigh of relief, knowing that their children have said a prayer to receive Jesus into their hearts. If they continues to follow the ways of this world, leading lives of waywardness and immorality, it could very well mean that they are not allowing the Holy Spirit to work out salvation in their hearts and minds. Under the Family Covenant we should claim their full salvation now in this life as well as their eternal salvation. In Psalm 112, it is written that the descendants of a man who fears the Lord will be mighty on earth and that the generation of the upright will be blessed! I want my children and grandchildren to be mighty on the earth and to be blessed by Almighty God!

The top priority in our prayers is that our children would receive a revelation of God the Father and His lovingkindness to them through the covenant. As we pray, we can ask the Lord to send laborers into our harvest field to bring the word of life to our unsaved or reprobate family members (Matthew 9:38). They will not believe if they do not hear, and only God knows who to send or what means will be effective to reach them. Ask the Holy Spirit to convict them and to visit them in dreams and visions or through an angel with a message. Since the devil is a thief, we need to forbid him to steal the word of truth once it is delivered. In the name of Jesus, we have the authority to destroy any negative influence of peers over our loved ones.

It is good to enter spiritual warfare for our families by praying out loud! Just as God spoke the world into being, so we can declare and proclaim the Word of God out loud in faith. It is a good thing for Satan to hear our audible prayers, and it is a good thing for us to hear what we are praying. The Bible says that faith comes from hearing ... and hearing by the Word of Christ (Romans 10:17). As we hear our own words, as we speak the words of the Scriptures, our own faith is strengthened.

God has given us so many wonderful promises for our families. When we pray the promises of God back to Him, He is delighted to answer them! In fact, He has said,

> So shall My word be that goes forth from My mouth; it shall not return void, but it shall accomplish what I please, and it shall prosper in the thing for which I sent it. (Isaiah 55:11)

He has also said, "I will contend with him who contends with you, and I will save your children" (Isaiah 49:25).

He has also said, "Behold, I give you the authority to trample on serpents and scorpions, and over all the power of the enemy, and nothing shall by any means hurt you" (Luke 10:19).

And He has said,

> As for Me, this is My covenant with them, says the Lord: My Spirit which is upon you, and My words which I have put in your mouth shall not depart from your mouth, nor from

the mouth of your children, nor from the mouth of your children's children, says the Lord, from now and forever. (Isaiah 59:21)

As we fight in prayer for our families, it is up to us to find His precious promises in the Scriptures and speak them back to Him. He has fulfilled every promise He has given to mankind through the history of the covenants, and He will fulfill every promise He has given to us for our families. It has been His desire since creation to have an intimate relationship with His people so that He could have many sons and daughters. It is my prayer that God will reveal His heart to you and that you will stand as Joshua did before His presence and proclaim, "As for me and my house, we will serve the Lord" (Joshua 24:15).

MY PRAYER IN CLOSING

Lord, thank You for revealing to us the mysteries and glories of Your covenants. As we read these words, we are grateful for the privilege of receiving these revelations for us and for our children.

"The secret things belong to the Lord our God, but those things which are revealed belong to us and to our children forever" (Deuteronomy 29:29).

Lord, I ask You to open the hearts and minds of each reader of this book in a powerful and personal way. Grant each one a spirit of wisdom and understanding of the knowledge of You and Your covenants so that they can truly experience Your love.

Father of Glory and God of our Lord Jesus Christ, give each one a special revelation of their calling such as You gave to Noah, Moses, Joshua, David, and Paul. Show them how important they are in Your plan for Your kingdom to come on earth as it is in heaven.

Holy Spirit, activate and illuminate these revelations into each life and each family so that the desire of the Father's heart will ultimately be realized when He gathers His sons and daughters to Himself on the last day.

In the name of Jesus *the Christ,*

Amen

ENDNOTES

1. Malcolm Smith, *The Lost Secret of the New Covenant*. Tulsa, OK: Harrison House, p. 24.

2. Francis Frangipane, *The Covenant-Keeping God*. The Elijah List & Breaking Christian News. http://www.elijahlist.com.

BIBLIOGRAPHY

Booker, Richard. *God's Blood Covenant*. Atlanta, GA: Cross Roads Books, 1979.

Hahn, Scott. *A Father Who Keeps His Promises*. Cincinnati OH: St. Anthony Messenger Press, 1998.

Hickey, Marilyn. *God's Covenant for Your Family*. Tulsa, OK: Harrison House, 1982.

Murray, Andrew. *How to Raise Your Children for Christ*. Minneapolis, MN: Bethany Fellowship, Inc., 1975.

Murray, Andrew. *The Believer's New Covenant*. Minneapolis, MN: Bethany House Publishers, 1984.

Prange, Erwin. *How to Pray for Your Children. (Family Covenant Praying)*. Minneapolis, MN: Bethany Fellowship Inc., 1979.

Shreve, Mike. *65 Promises from God for Your Child*. Lake Mary, FL: Charisma House, 2013.

Smith, Malcolm. *The Lost Secret of the New Covenant*. Tulsa, OK: Harrison House, 2002.

Trumbull, H. Clay. *The Blood Covenant*. Kirkwood MO: Impact Books, Inc., 1975.

ONLINE RESOURCES

Biggs, Charles R. "God's Covenant House: A Sketch of God's Construction Project." http://www. aplacefortruth.org. 2012.

Deffinbaugh, Bob. "The Call of Abraham." http://bible.org. 1012.

Downey, Dan. "Believing God for Our Children." http://www. savedhealed.com.

Frangipagne, Francis. "Those Who Make a Covenant with God." www. frangipagne.org. 2011.

Fruchtenbaum, Dr. Arnold. "The Eight Covenants of the Bible." http.//www.messianicassociation.org. 2012.

Goheen, Michael W. "Reading the Bible as One Story." http:// catalystresources.org.

Hall, Wes. "The Message of the Manger." IHOP-KC Mission Base. www.ihop.org.

Hanko, Rev.Ronald. "God's Covenant, a Family Covenant." http// www.reformed Alberta.ca 1012.

Lane, Fr. Tommy. "God's Plan for the Family—A Reflection of God's Love." http://www.Frtommylane.com 2013.

Lee, Jeanniene. "It Happened at the Cross." http://www. changetheimageministries.org. 2013.

Linsley, Alice C. "The Scarlet Cord Woven Through the Bible." http://jandyongenesis. blogspot.com 2008.

Marshall, Graemme. "The Scarlet Cord: Echoes of the Passover." http.//www.reformedalberta.ca. 2012.

Morgan, Philip. "A Lamb for a House" by Andrew Murray. http:// Philmorgan.org 2012.

Naugle, Dr. David. "Jesus Christ and the Kingdom of God." http:// www. colsoncenter.org. 2013.

Nelson, Wayne. "Understanding the Blood Covenant." www. faithwriters.com. 2011.

Piper, John. "The Conquest of Canaan." http://www.desiringgod. org. 2013.

Roberts, Dr. Mark. "What was the Message of Jesus?" http://www. patheos.com.

Schlebusch, Adi. "The Importance of Lineage in God's Covenant." http://faithandheritage.com. 2013.

Sliker, David. "God's Covenant With Abraham." IHOP-KC Mission Base. www.ihop.org.

Sliker, David. "God's Covenant With David–the Kingdom of God." IHOP-KC Mission Base. www.ihop.org.

Smith, Rev. Ralph A. "The Noahic Covenant." http://www.ovrlnd.com 2011.

Steward, Katie. "Promises for Our Children in the Lord." http://www.whatsaiththescripture.com. 2013.

Versteeg, Rev. Bill. "Covenant and Family." www.pbv.thunder-bay.on.ca. 2011.

Wilson, Dr. Ralph. "The Covenant of Circumcision with Abraham." http://www.jesuswalk.com. 2012.

Wood, Bryant. "The Walls of Jericho." http://www.answersingenesis.org. 2012.

Woods, Dr. Andy. "The Prophetic Significance of the Davidic Line and Covenant." http://www.bibleprophecyblog.com. 2013.

CPSIA information can be obtained at www.ICGtesting.com
Printed in the USA
BVOW05s1207150414

350627BV00003B/3/P